VISUAL LEAP

VISUAL LEAP

A Step-by-Step Guide to
VISUAL LEARNING
for Teachers and Students

JESSE BERG, MSIT, MEd

Lamprey & Lee
an imprint of Bibliomotion, Inc.

First published in 2015 by Lamprey & Lee, an imprint of Bibliomotion, Inc.
39 Harvard Street
Brookline, MA 02445
Tel: 617-934-2427
www.bibliomotion.com

Printed in the United States of America

ISBN 978-1-942108-07-8 - print
ISBN 978-1-942108-08-5 - ebook

[CIP data has been applied for]

This book is dedicated to everyone who has ever needed a go-to strategy to solve a problem, think more clearly, learn something new, or communicate a complicated idea. It is dedicated to the vast effort we put into teaching, learning, planning, getting out in front of our ideas, breaking down the barriers to achievement, and accomplishing our goals, whatever they may be. The future rides on our ability to think, learn, and create. This book is dedicated to making it easier for us to reach our destinations.

CONTENTS

PREFACE

I believe with all my heart that visual thinking can change lives. Why do I believe this? Because it has changed my life, and I am just like millions of other people with ideas who struggle to develop and execute them. For me, and for a vast number of smart and creative people, the simple *visual thinking* strategies outlined in this book can transform our ability to produce in the world, realize dreams, and solve problems, no matter how complex. If these strategies work for you like they have worked for me, I promise that your intellectual confidence will grow by leaps, bolstered by your enhanced ability to organize and develop your ideas, plan a course of action, and accomplish your goals.

Writing this book has been the most difficult—and most terrifying—thing I have ever done. However, I feel compelled by the need to share these ideas. My fear stems from two things: (1) dying with regret and (2) my proclivity to do things 90 percent—the first 90 percent. I am not blessed with willpower and perseverance. I embrace distraction. I love immediate gratification . . . and frequent breaks. I hate grit. Despite these tendencies, I was driven to finish this book because its very content made it possible for me to embark upon and complete this monumental task. Finishing it is a huge relief, and failing to do so would have been a haunting regret.

The process of visual thinking—which I used to write this book and which I explain in these pages—is the most important thing I have to teach. If you are reading this book, half of my mission is complete. However, if taking the Visual Leap helps you or your students, then my bucket will truly be filled.

INTRODUCTION

Why You? Why Now?

This book is geared primarily toward K–12 educators, though, more broadly, it is for anyone who needs a go-to strategy for learning, problem solving, and organizing ideas. It focuses on the needs of teachers because, more than anyone else, they are the ones with the opportunity to provide our next generation with the skills needed to navigate and succeed in an ever-changing world, a world where the life span of useful knowledge is perpetually decreasing and the need to learn, adapt, and retool is constant.

Visual Leap explains how to think visually and how to teach the skill of visual thinking to others. The explicit, step-by-step method it delivers is effective and easy to master because it matches how human beings naturally learn. Visual thinking skills enhance intellectual curiosity and academic perseverance by providing a framework to help students remember, analyze, and create. Since it is a thinking strategy, the approach is applicable to learning virtually any type of idea or academic content, and it universally helps students improve reading comprehension, write more effectively, and even listen better.

Beyond teaching specific skills, however, this book aims to help people learn how to think for themselves. The ultimate goal is to nourish students with strategies they can use independently in diverse situations when the questions they have to solve are open-ended and have no clear-cut right or wrong answers. In addition, if you or your students would benefit from writing more efficiently, learning more easily, or solving problems more creatively, then this book is for you.

We need this book now because more than half of the people in our society are vastly underserved by their education. I am not referring (at this time) to the problem of underfunded schools or the politics of education. The prosperity of our society is built on innovation, collaboration, and creativity—on noticing opportunity in the gaps of what exists and in seeing entirely undiscovered horizons—yet the way we teach often stifles these critical forces. At the societal level, this has an impact that I will leave for the economists to debate. At the individual level, though, the entrenched traditional ways of teaching have a detrimental impact on millions of children who never learn how to harness their creative and independent thinking.

The problem is that the millions of people who predominately think visually were not taught learning strategies that match how they think, nor were they taught with methods that match how they learn best. This disconnect has dire consequences. For individuals, it makes learning vastly harder than it has to be. Debilitating school experiences can push students into a downward spiral of frustration and shame, often leading to low self-esteem and professional underachievement that hurts families and communities. On a societal level, the impact compounds dramatically. Many of these disenfranchised students who flounder in school are precisely the innovative, creative types who have the potential to discover novel things, see unique opportunities, and invent new ways of solving problems.

Not all of these learners fail. The annals of business are filled with examples of entrepreneurs who attribute their success to dyslexia. Billionaire dropout Richard Branson of Virgin Atlantic is nearly as famous for his ADHD as he is for his award-winning hair. Many of the success stories have a common thread: the individual was frustrated in school, couldn't learn or perform tasks the way he or she was shown, was forced to discover the road less traveled (or not traveled at all), and used the pain of school as motivation to persevere. It's a glorious story (which I am trying to live myself), but where does it leave the people with less luck, less support, or less grit, or those who simply don't stumble onto their magical yellow brick road?

I am qualified to propose a path for this group because (in addition to my education and experience) this group is my group. Their problem is my problem. For me, learning has always been a slow, difficult, solitary journey. As a student, and even through college and my early career, I never learned tools or strategies that matched my thinking processes and helped me accomplish my goals. For much of my life, it has been inordinately difficult to organize my ideas and finish virtually any complex cognitive task. I am creative, clever, and skilled in a lot of ways; I am also distractible, forgetful, impulsive, and often oblivious. As for character traits, I love change and hate repetition. Academically, I forget what I read so quickly that it barely seems worth the effort, and while I write well, the task is so overwhelming that I'd avoid it entirely if I could. A lot of these struggles stem from the fact that I have a hard time getting started and sticking to a plan (or making a good plan from the get-go). Like many, I am a divergent thinker, a visual learner, a "right-brain-oriented" person. My mind spirals around ideas, sometimes homing in on them, other times hurling them out into orbit. I don't drive straight toward the finish line; I meander. I am a nonlinear thinker. This is both a blessing and curse.

I am also a teacher. I went into teaching with a strong motivation to make learning easier for others like me. I started my career in education as a Spanish teacher. I didn't know how I would make learning easier, but I had empathy for struggling students and a humanistic and constructivist philosophy of education, forged first during my progressive high school experience (at Germantown Friends School in Philadelphia) and galvanized while earning my master's degree in education from Temple University (thanks to the late Dr. Gertrude Moskowitz, author of *Caring and Sharing in the Foreign Language Classroom*).

A seminal moment in my professional life, which I now see provided the original seed of this book, occurred in a graduate class at Philadelphia University, where I was getting my second master's degree, in instructional technology. The instructor briefly demonstrated Inspiration Software, which she used to diagram an idea. The demo was only about twenty minutes, but lightning struck. I had never seen anything like it. She created a rudimentary visual map of an idea by moving around symbols and words like puzzle pieces. At the time I had no idea what this would mean for my future, but I realized immediately that my mind had just been unlocked. Ideas could be organized visually!

From that moment, my career has focused on delving into visual thinking and learning, and on following that specialty on whatever path it led me. Over the years I have worked with visual thinking as a Spanish teacher, as a computer teacher, as a staff developer in education, and now as the founder of Visual Leap, LLC. My life's work—and the mission of this book—is to teach others explicit ways to think visually in order to make learning easier. My goal, and my hope, is that the strategies presented here—which helped me to start, write, and finish this book—will help unleash some of the vast human potential that is currently stifled in the countless number of people who struggle to fully realize their ideas. If we can put the right tools and thinking strategies into their hands, we can release a wave of innovation and creativity that benefits not only those individuals, but all of society.

PART 1

Understanding the Visual Leap

"Visual Leap" is a metaphor and a prescription for a desperately needed shift in education. "Leap" symbolizes a transformation in the way we need to teach children, by refocusing on critical thinking and independent learning. "Visual" describes the type of strategies that our system must incorporate and promote. When I thought about it further, I realized that "leap" is also an acronym that stands for "learn, earn, achieve, perform." I believe that these are the types of positive outcomes that we can expect from individuals who know how to use visual thinking strategically and deliberately.

Human beings possess a natural ability to think visually; it developed throughout our evolution and exists in the wiring of our brains. The purpose of this book is to provide a road map that helps teachers convey to students how to use this innate ability to make all kinds of learning easier and therefore maximize their intellectual potential. For students who learn these strategies, the tools may mean the difference between graduating and dropping out of school or college. For professionals—both teachers and students who have left school—the strategies become a set of tools for problem solving, innovating, and collaborating effectively. I challenge you to experiment with the methods and strategies in this book. Adapt them to your students' needs and make them your own. It takes time, trust, and practice to add new tools to your teaching and learning toolkit, but these techniques are intuitive and surprisingly easy.

Visual Leap fits squarely in the constructivist camp long embraced by major educational organizations, including the Association for Supervision and Curriculum Development (ASCD), Center for Applied Special Technology (CAST), and International Society for Technology in Education (ISTE). Visual Leap strategies embody the central goal of the Common Core State Standards, which is to prepare students to be flexible thinkers who can reason, write, communicate, and adapt to the professional demands of an exciting and unpredictable future.

Chapter 1 discusses visual learning and introduces the term **visual inquiry**. Chapter 2 presents the cognitive science that forms the underpinning of the visual thinking strategies presented throughout the book. Chapter 3 explores the implications and imperatives of utilizing visual learning methods in the classroom.

Thank you for embarking on this journey with me. Let's jump in!

CHAPTER 1

Visual Inquiry

How many times have you heard a person mention that she is a "visual learner"? This phrase means different things to different people, but to some degree all people are visual learners. The human brain is hardwired to think and learn visually. Our minds are pattern-seeking machines. This incredible mental asset makes the human brain the perfect tool for creativity and complex problem solving. We use our innate visual ability when we analyze and infer through observation and when we construct new objects by looking to see how others are built. It is possible, however, to use very similar visual processes to analyze ideas, understand concepts, communicate effectively, and even to write. This presents a powerful opportunity to make learning easier and more intuitive.

Consciously and strategically using our innate visual thinking ability to learn is a process I call **visual inquiry**. For our purposes, visual inquiry refers to a set of strategies that centers on the skill of creating meaningful, organized visual representations of ideas and concepts using webs and maps that show how ideas fit together. This book provides a step-by-step approach that explains how to do it, offers strategies for integrating visual inquiry into the classroom, and illustrates how to teach the skill to others. If we, as educators, can successfully transfer this skill to our students, we can transform learning.

Visual inquiry refers to a set of strategies that centers on the skill of creating meaningful, organized visual representations of ideas and concepts using webs and maps.

These visualizations can incorporate image, text, and spatial relationships. In some cases, depending on the tools used to make them, they can even utilize sound. Representations can be created with pencil and paper or with software, and with practice, they can be developed in the mind's eye. The goal of visual inquiry is to allow the learner to analyze and represent information in an organized fashion so that it can be fully understood, evaluated, and analyzed. Visual inquiry is a highly creative process that involves free association, pattern recognition, and critical thinking. Though flexible, visual inquiry can be taught as a process that follows explicit guidelines, thus making it easy to teach, master, and use in diverse educational settings.

The most effective visual learning occurs when students create visualizations that follow a few broad principles and adhere to clear rules. Students can create diagrams collaboratively in groups, with teachers, or individually. The ideal workspace for visual thinking allows students to *freely manipulate ideas like puzzle pieces*. Many of my preferred tools for visual learning involve technology. Software programs such as Inspiration, apps such as Idea Flip, and web tools like Popplet—which allow users to combine pictures, text, and arrows to show visual relationships—are very good for this purpose, but so is pencil and paper. Most of the diagrams in this book were created using Inspiration Software, which is commonly used in many schools. In the resources section at the end of the book, you'll find additional suggestions for software, apps, and books about visual thinking and learning.

As we will see more clearly in the chapters to come, using image, text, shape, and, in some cases, sound enables learners to take a nonlinear approach to thinking that utilizes the whole mind and matches the way human beings think and solve problems in the real world. We will prove this by visually mapping this process as it occurs in human communication. In doing so, we will identify the rules that govern this universally human way of learning and teach students how to apply those rules for diverse purposes. As teachers, we will know we have reached our goal of teaching students to think visually when they are able to diagram ideas for themselves and use those strategies independently. Then we will know we have given them a skill for life.

How Visual Learning Helps Students

Visual thinking has clear benefits in many curricular and skill development areas for students. According to analysis conducted by the Institute for the Advancement of Research in Education,[1] visual learning techniques improve students' ability to:

- Organize and analyze information
- Integrate new knowledge
- Clarify their thoughts
- Think critically
- Write with proficiency
- Retain information
- Comprehend what they are reading
- Understand and solve mathematical problems

That list is compelling, but the benefits are even more basic. Visual inquiry provides a universal strategy for conceptualizing a problem. It helps learners see the big picture and analyze the evidence. For this reason, visual thinking helps at every phase of learning—from approaching a problem and developing a plan to seeing a project through to completion. This skill facilitates a learner's ability to monitor her own progress and stay on track—or to get back on track when she gets derailed. Visual thinking decreases procrastination and increases perseverance. It helps the learner create a plan and provides a path for follow-through (fig. 1.1).

Students using visual thinking strategies learn to "see" their ideas develop and get a holistic picture of the entire scope of an idea, so they can more easily reflect on and assess their own thinking. Diagramming ideas—rather than writing them in sentence form—lets learners

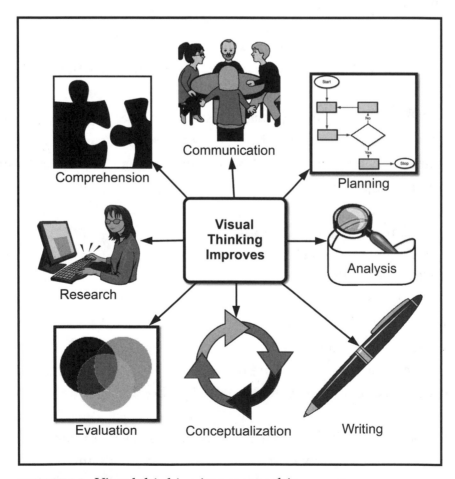

FIGURE 1.1. Visual thinking improves achievement.

evaluate the strengths, weaknesses, sequence, and gaps in an argument without the distraction of punctuation, grammar, and spelling. For this reason, visual thinking is one of the most direct and powerful meta-cognitive strategies around.

Mastering the process of visual inquiry will shave hours from students' writing because it allows them to clarify their ideas before they begin to write. They will know their arguments are complete because they will see how ideas are connected. This method will allow them to organize and evaluate complex ideas and reveal relationships and patterns.

Working with ideas using a combination of image, space, and text helps students remember and assimilate information more effectively than when they simply see it written or hear it described. As students learn to represent ideas by combining multiple modalities—visual, spatial, textual, and auditory—they will make more connections, better understand relationships, and recall more information. Learning to think visually helps students become more creative, efficient, and effective learners. At all ages, whether as young children working on prewriting exercises or as older students tackling multifaceted projects and research papers, students can use visual inquiry to make complex tasks more manageable.

How Visual Learning Helps Teachers

Visual strategies help teachers as much as they help students. Why? Most students are comfortable learning visually, and when they are taught to think through problems in ways that engage their visual intelligence, they learn more easily. This book provides a simple method of working with content in order to make it accessible to students. As a benefit for the teacher, lesson planning becomes easier and faster, and classroom dialogue flourishes. When you begin to challenge students to think about problems visually, your teacher talk time will decrease and constructive student dialogue will increase.

Visual inquiry puts the messy job of learning squarely in the lap of students. Unlike teaching stalwarts like PowerPoint presentations, which are time-consuming to create and tend to put students in the passive role of recipient of information, visual strategies do the opposite. They thrust students into the role of the active learner who makes connections, pieces together understanding, and reaps the lasting benefit of assimilating new knowledge and learning how to learn. If this sounds scary or difficult, think again. It might well be the easiest and most impactful change you ever make to your teaching practice.

> When you begin to challenge students to think about problems visually, your teacher talk time will decrease and constructive student dialogue will increase.

All students benefit from teaching that engages them in multiple ways. Visual inquiry methods offer a simple and effective strategy for reaching those students who learn best by working actively with information in multiple modalities that engage the whole mind. This group includes gifted students, students with ADHD or dyslexia, those on the autism spectrum, emerging readers and writers, and students functioning below grade level. These strategies support kinesthetic learners who thrive from direct interaction with content, visual-spatial learners who think primarily in pictures, as well as all types of divergent, nonlinear thinkers who need strategies to help them see relationships and make connections as they learn. The benefits of visual techniques are not limited to at-risk students. More traditional, auditory-sequential learners profit because these methods develop new thinking skills that strengthen less-used neural pathways. By augmenting their ability to think creatively, learn independently, and communicate ideas with others, they become more well-rounded, effective, and flexible thinkers.

Types of Visual Thinking

Visual thinking is individualistic—to a degree. Making meaningful representations of ideas requires learners to apply their own background knowledge, experience in the world, and personal preferences. However, universal rules guide the visual thinking process. There are many formats for visual thinking and different names for each type. In *Visual Leap*, we will focus primarily on a family of graphic organizers that includes **semantic webs** (also known as **idea maps**), **mind maps**, and **tree diagrams**.

These organizers are grouped together because, at their core, they share a powerful visual literacy related to the way they depict the hierarchy of information and link ideas. For this reason, they are especially effective in simplifying complex academic tasks like writing. The organizers also share some rigid rules, which make them easy to teach and use.

Perhaps the most incredible thing about these organizers is that they simultaneously enable the mind to work *visually* and *linearly*, fully engaging both cerebral hemispheres for a truly whole-brain learning experience. We will explore this concept in detail, but suffice it to say, these amazing visual structures allow the mind to work at peak strength because they provide a net that catches ideas exactly the way the mind processes them.

Following are images of this family of graphic organizers that show the similarities and differences between them (figs. 1.2–1.5).

Figure 1.2 is a **semantic web**, also known as an **idea map**. Both names are used in educational writing, and for our purposes, they are one and the same. The **mind map** (fig. 1.3) is a variant with branches rather than connecting arrows, but these two graphic organizers structure information in essentially the same way. They share a centrally placed node in the middle of the form and branch out from there. Branches can split

Visual Leap

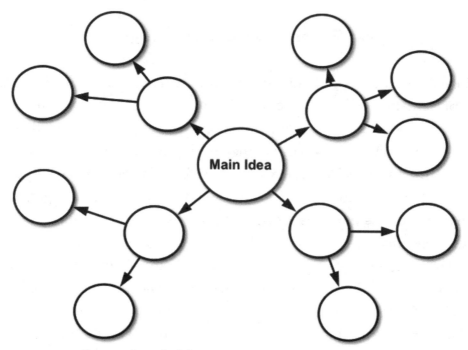

FIGURE 1.2. Semantic web/idea map.

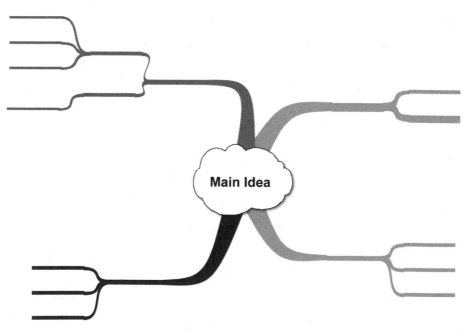

FIGURE 1.3. Mind map.

indefinitely, enabling them to represent highly complex ideas in a clear, hierarchical way. Their ability to show a concept from main idea to the smallest detail of a detail is essential to the powerful visual literacy they convey.

British author and renowned thought leader Tony Buzan popularized the term "mind map," and he coined the term "radial thinking" to represent the way ideas branch out from a main topic. Mind mapping is a well-established practice worldwide in education and in the corporate sector. In the United States, semantic webs, or "webbing," are more common in educational settings. I use the terms somewhat interchangeably because both offer a similar structure for the practice of visual inquiry.

The **tree diagram** (fig. 1.4) is a first cousin to the semantic web and mind map. It is different because the main idea is usually at the top, not in the middle. However, if you examine the way it branches out from the main topic into subtopics and details, it is clear that the tree diagram fits in this group. Plus, when the tree diagram is reoriented—into a **split tree**—its similarity to semantic webs and mind maps becomes perfectly clear (fig. 1.5). Organizational charts and family trees are often depicted in this way.

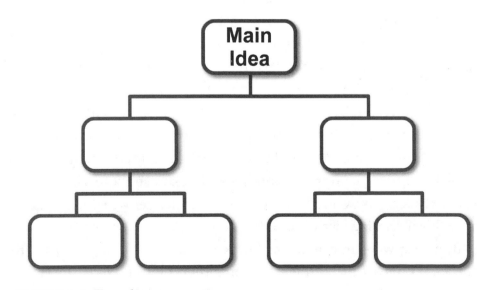

FIGURE 1.4. Tree diagram.

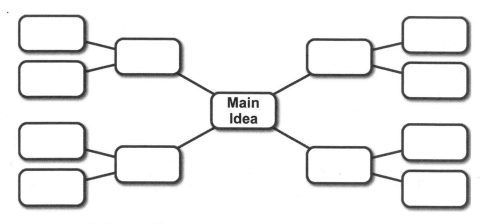

FIGURE 1.5. Split tree diagram.

Elementary and middle-school teachers have been using these diagrams for decades, usually as handouts. This practice has merit, but printed graphic organizers force students to sandwich their ideas into the pre-made shapes prescribed by the organizer. These types of diagrams are most often used as a way to define a concept, such as a hexagon or the traits of a character. However, only the simplest ideas can be represented on a printout with pre-established blanks. Confining thinking to these small shapes restricts students' ability to expand on their ideas and learn independently.

In part 2 of the book we will transform these diagrams into something more dynamic and powerful by identifying and analyzing the underlying visual rules that govern them as a framework for mapping out any concept. These rules have the potential to revolutionize the way we harness creativity, listen, and write. In part 3 we will apply these universal principles in ways that enable learners to deconstruct information to reveal a concept's skeletal structure, with dramatic implications for reading comprehension. We will also use these same laws to teach students how to construct new knowledge, which can change how they organize ideas and write.

By using webs and maps as blank slates for thinking, we flip the equation on teaching. Students become their own teachers, and teachers transform from provider of knowledge to co-learner and facilitator.

When you flip this one big switch, students become critical thinkers and curators of knowledge. They gain a way to tackle any problem or attack any question. When students master the skill of constructing ideas visually, their maps become blueprints for any outcome they desire or any assignment their teacher requires, whether it's an essay, poster, oral argument, podcast, or movie.

> When students master the skill of constructing ideas visually, their maps become blueprints for any outcome they desire or any assignment their teacher requires, whether it's an essay, poster, oral argument, podcast, or movie.

Webs and their graphic cousins are not the only forms of visual thinking, but they are without question some of the most flexible and universal for adding structure to creative ideas and enabling learners to work effectively with those ideas. They are the right place to start for a lifetime of visual thinking because of their clear rules and broad applications. After students master webbing and can visualize ideas, they will be empowered to dig into hard questions and express innovative ideas. Their contribution may be to reveal a novel relationship, explore an elusive question, or answer a question that has not yet been asked.

The essence of visual inquiry involves finding a logical way to represent an idea. The goal is to show how the information fits together spatially, through relationships, using as few words as possible. When webs and maps are used for visual inquiry, they become invaluable tools for writing and planning. The process isn't always easy. Unpacking a complex idea can feel like archaeology, but once an idea can be pieced together and connected in a form that makes sense, it can be owned and controlled. When students begin to think about problems, ideas, prompts, and questions as things that can be analyzed in a process of visual inquiry, they will have taken the Visual Leap.

CHAPTER 2

Why Visual Inquiry Works

Visual inquiry works for powerful reasons that go to the heart of the way human beings process information. It engages the whole mind like a magical net that lets us catch ideas as fast as we can generate them and keep them captured until we figure out how they fit into the grand scope of the concept (fig. 2.1). This approach simultaneously allows

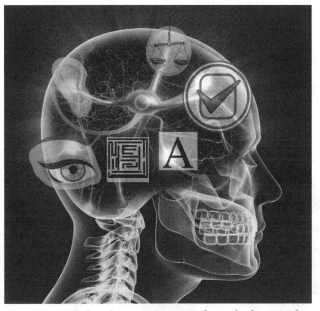

FIGURE 2.1. Visual thinking engages the whole mind.

learners to process an idea holistically and to work sequentially to organize its parts, like puzzle pieces, experimenting and playing with them until we see how they fit together. Sometimes we use logic to work with ideas. Other times we look for patterns. In the natural course of thinking, humans constantly toggle back and forth between these two processes. Visual inquiry is a deliberate and conscious strategy built on what the brain does best—find patterns, identify gaps, make associations, and plan actions. Visual inquiry lets us see ideas as they develop and evaluate and revise the concept as we construct it.

The magical net and jigsaw puzzle comparison is more than a metaphor. Visual inquiry is a method of learning that stands firmly on a foundation of cognitive learning theory and what we currently know about how neural networks function. Activity in the brain is electrical. Impulses travel through the brain, from neuron to neuron, via major neural networks and through a brainscape with limitless possibilities. The path is not linear. Any one neuron can send electrical signals simultaneously in different directions to as many as ten thousand neighboring neurons, where impulses are interpreted by specialized modules spread throughout the brain.[1]

> Visual inquiry is a method of learning that stands firmly on a foundation of cognitive learning theory and what we currently know about how neural networks function.

The scientific underpinning of visual inquiry draws on our knowledge of the three primary neural networks of the brain and long-standing cognitive learning theories. These networks are the **recognition networks, affective networks,** and **strategic networks.**[2] Interplay between them is the focus of the Universal Design for Learning (UDL) framework developed by the Center for Applied Special Technology (CAST). Visual inquiry methods also rest on the shoulders of constructivist cognitive learning theories including **schema theory, dual coding theory,** and **cognitive load theory.** The practice of visual inquiry fosters successful learning experiences.

How Learning Happens: Neural Networks and Learning Theories at Play

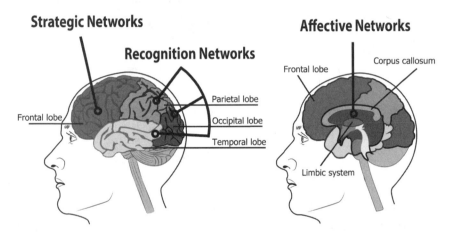

FIGURE 2.2. The three primary neural networks.

Learning is a complex, interconnected process that involves the whole brain. CAST has articulated a simple way to understand learning, which it developed through twenty-five years of research. At the most general level, the brain's three primary cognitive networks (each with many sub-networks) govern the way humans recognize information, evaluate it, and execute actions. The interplay between these networks enables us to function in the world.[3] By studying these broad neural networks, we can find what amounts to a "neural address" for where and how learning happens.

We will focus on two different regions of the brain—the cerebral cortex and the limbic system—because the recognition, strategic, and affective networks correspond to these regions. The brain also has two distinct hemispheres, which are similar in structure, but which process information in profoundly different ways. Connecting the two hemispheres and the limbic system is the corpus callosum, which serves as a multidirectional superhighway, sending massive amounts of information (in the form of tiny electrical impulses) between the two hemispheres and the limbic system in an integrated flow of communication that is interpreted and acted upon. The differences between right-brain and left-brain thinking have dominated much of the research and discussion about learning for at least a generation, and visual inquiry provides a way to actively engage the strengths of both hemispheres in the learning process.

The Recognition Networks

The recognition networks encompass the **parietal**, **occipital**, and **temporal lobes** of the **cerebral cortex** (fig. 2.2). They enable us to identify all types of sensory information, including images, sounds, smells, spatial information, and touch. They also allow us to recognize patterns and formulate rules to create a hierarchy of information that indexes the sensory data we receive. These rules and generalizations allow us to perceive the world around us with a great degree of accuracy. Such capability has always been essential for survival. Sensory recognition helps us, for example, to determine a threat, identify food, and even find a good mate. It also plays a critical part in academic achievement by building patterns around information. Through experience, these patterns increase and enhance our ability to recognize and use knowledge in increasingly complex ways.[4]

> Sensory recognition helps us to determine a threat, identify food, and even find a good mate—and it also plays a critical part in academic achievement.

Developmental psychologist Jean Piaget was one of the earliest learning theorists to use the term **schemas**, or **schemata**, to describe the building blocks of knowledge that children use to organize, remember, recall, and construct information. According to Piaget and subsequent developmental and educational psychologists, schemas are patterns of thought that organize categories of information, and they are continually reworked, refined, and enhanced as new experiences are added.[5] For example, a young child learning language may point to any picture of a four-legged animal and call it a dog. However, as that child has more experiences, such as petting a dog, hearing one bark, or gaining contrasting experiences with cats and cows, the "dog" schema becomes more refined, and the concept becomes a part of that person's long-term memory. The more developed the schema, the more effectively it can be recalled and used to construct new knowledge.

The recognition networks are highly specialized to build schemas by finding patterns and making rules out of the sensory information they receive. In fact, there may be as many as twenty-five hundred specialized modules in each hemisphere. These modules are located in discrete physical locations in the occipital lobe at the rear of the cortex, and each one has a specific role in recognizing color, shape, motion, depth, line orientation, texture, and every other different type of visual information.[6] Auditory information and speech comprehension are processed in their own specialized modules in the temporal lobe.

The image shown in figure 2.3 used positron emission tomography (PET) to capture a brain exposed to a set of words under different conditions—seeing words, hearing words, reading Braille, and thinking.[7] The highlighted portions show where activity is occurring, to what degree, and under which condition: the occipital lobe is active when the individual sees words, the temporal lobe when the subject hears words, the parietal lobe while touching (Braille), and the frontal lobe while thinking.

This PET scan shows clearly that recognition is *distributed* across the cortex by the module designed to handle the specific type of input.

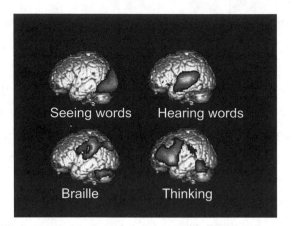

Seeing words   Hearing words

Braille   Thinking

FIGURE 2.3. Sight, hearing, Braille, thinking. Colored positron emission tomography (PET) scans of areas of the human brain activated by different tasks.

But the story does not stop there. Recognition happens in *parallel*, not sequentially. **Parallel processing** allows multiple areas of the cortex to receive sensory information simultaneously. Therefore, we are able to see, hear, feel, and smell stimuli at the same time. The more recognition modules that are stimulated simultaneously, the greater the activity of the brain as a whole. The impact of engaging multiple modules in the brain has major implications for teaching and learning. When students interact with material in ways that use more regions of the brain, learning becomes easier.

Dual coding theory (DCT) complements schema theory and provides a research basis for the concept of multisensory learning for reading and writing. A basic assumption of DCT is that our brain codes information in two primary ways—verbally and nonverbally—that enable us to understand and communicate ideas. Verbal coding helps us to understand ideas through language, oral communication, and text, while nonverbal coding allows us to understand and learn through mental imagery.[8] DCT asserts that the right hemisphere of the brain is more specialized for visual and holistic thinking, while the left brain more efficiently handles auditory information, language, and linear processes. Studies testing DCT have found that when content is delivered in both visual and auditory modalities it is more easily recalled and more effectively used. This makes sense in light of schema theory. Working with information that is coded in multiple modalities adds to an individual's schematic representation of the idea and should make that idea easier to understand.[9]

It is well established that when we provide conditions for students that stimulate multiple areas of the brain simultaneously, recall improves. Students remember best when they see an image, see the text, hear a definition, and have an example that gives context to the information.[10] Dual coding theory provides a research basis for multisensory learning and a compelling argument that all learners benefit from teaching that includes verbal and visual representations, which inherently engage both sides of the brain. We transform this principle into practice through visual inquiry.

The Affective Networks

The **affective networks** are located in the limbic system, which is beneath the cerebrum and in the center of the brain. The limbic system is a more ancient part of the neural system and is considered part of the "unconscious brain." It evolved along with mammals and plays a significant role in long-term memory.[11] The affective networks attribute emotional coding to information. They can trigger reactions such as fight, flee, wait and see, or good things are about to happen to me. Affective networks are responsible for instinctual physiological reactions to stimuli, such as adrenaline rushes, muscle contractions, gut feelings, and human attraction.

The affective networks act as a gateway for information between instinctual behavior and strategic, conscious action. Let's work through an example:

CRASH! You hear a loud sound.
FREEZE. You tense your muscles and freeze in place.
RECOVER. You realize it was just a pot clanging to the ground
and you relax.

In this simple and common event, several cognitive processes transpired. You had a subconscious, reflexive response to a loud auditory stimulus that was processed in the limbic system by a module specialized to assign a first response for auditory stimulation: you froze. Then, perhaps a quarter-second later, the recognition networks identified the sound as a pot falling to the ground. The affective networks then recategorized the event as nonthreatening. That allowed the stimulus to be processed by the strategic networks, which gave you the green light to move on with what you had been doing.

The affective networks have developed such that most people have similar reactions to threatening events, but there are significant differences in people's affective cognitive wiring—differences that have an impact on teaching and learning. While most people experience fear when confronted with a frothing, unleashed Rottweiler, human beings react with a wide degree of emotional difference in less dramatic circumstances. For instance, in a traffic jam, some people fill with rage, and others sit in resigned boredom.

For children in school, the reaction of the affective networks can determine whether they engage in the learning process or shut down. A student who experiences debilitating anxiety during a pop quiz will not be able to show what she knows. In contrast, a learner who becomes alert at the prospect of a pop quiz may enter a state of readiness that heightens her ability to perform. For one distracted student, a teacher's "hairy eyeball" serves as a nonverbal reminder to get back on track. A different student might interpret the same look of disapproval as a type of threat or as evidence that the teacher "hates" him, and he may shut down. Students, like all people, exhibit a range of responses to a given stimulus, and the affective networks will have much influence over this.

The affective networks, while primitive and instinctual, are an essential gateway for learning. Affective health can lead learners to overcome challenges and succeed. In studies of highly successful dyslexics, researchers have concluded that a high degree of engagement in a subject matter can allow these learners to push through obstacles erected by weaknesses in the strategic and recognition networks.[12] Unfortunately, the opposite is often the case. Learners with deficits in these areas who have negative academic experiences are more likely to shut down in school. Their feelings about learning and the emotions that school elicits interfere with achievement.

The affective networks are critical to learning because they manage our responses to feelings like excitement, curiosity, and fear. They provide the emotional state that is either conducive to learning or that stops learning in its tracks. As teachers, we need to use this knowledge to design instruction that allows learners to engage with material more fully, in ways that are authentic and genuine. To accomplish this, we must be sensitive and responsive to the emotional needs of our students and engage them meaningfully in the process of learning. Interventions may be as simple as allowing students to focus on reading in their areas of interest, offering assignments that have elements of choice, and honoring student preferences for assessments; conversely, it may mean defining requirements explicitly for students who prefer a more rigid structure. However we do it, if we want to help students learn, we need them to care.

> As teachers, we need to use our understanding of the affective networks to design instruction that allows learners to engage with material more fully, in ways that are authentic and genuine.

The Strategic Networks

The **strategic networks** are located in the frontal lobe of the cerebral cortex and are the locus of conscious thought. Known as the "conscious brain," the frontal lobe is the most recent part of the brain to evolve. It is where higher-order thinking occurs. The complexity and sophistication of the frontal lobe is uniquely human, and it allows our species to engage in complex thinking, including problem solving, verbal communication, and self-awareness. This part of the brain evolved rapidly approximately 1.5 million years ago, as evidenced by fossil records from skulls of that period. This was an epoch of dramatic planetary climate change that would have required innovative strategies for survival. During this time our hominid ancestors made tools, lived socially, and hunted in groups. Though we cannot with relative certainty date early language to more than fifty thousand to one hundred thousand years ago, evolutionary changes in the frontal lobe and skull suggest that language could have begun to evolve well over a million years ago.[13]

The strategic networks are responsible for integrating and managing the information they receive from the recognition and affective networks and using that information to formulate plans, learn, and solve problems. The higher-order thinking conducted in the frontal lobe comprises a series of essential skills known as **executive function**. Executive function can be considered the mind's manager. It regulates such critical behaviors as organization, time management, and planning. Executive function is critical to learning because it allows people to regulate their behavior and integrate and use new information.

Cognitive load theory and the concept of **working memory** are closely related to executive function. They provide an explanation of how the strategic networks function and illuminate their limitations. Cognitive load theory asserts that there is a maximum amount of information that people can manage at one time before reaching a mental saturation point. In other words, there is a maximum number of ideas that the mind can manipulate at a given time. This amount is called working memory.

Working memory is the ability to keep information "online" for a short period of time. One way to think about working memory is the "number of balls" a learner can juggle in his mind before forgetting something or losing concentration. It is crucial for reading, writing, arithmetic, and complex problem solving. Working memory allows the learner to maintain a train of thought and block out external distraction. We can also think about it like a game of pinball. Pinball, for those who don't remember, is an arcade game that consists of a metal ball, flippers, and bumpers. The goal is to keep the ball in play on the tilted board. The most successful players are able to keep the ball bouncing between the bumpers toward the top of the table. When the ball starts to roll down, timely flicks of the flippers can send it back up. A pinball machine with a lot of bumpers and flippers makes it easier to keep the ball in play.

This is quite similar to the way a person works with a complicated idea (with working memory being the bumpers and flippers). An individual with strong working memory can keep the idea bouncing around in her mind, block out distractions, and follow it through to its logical conclusion. For students with working memory deficits, however, managing a complex idea is like playing pinball on a table with no bumpers and only one set of flippers. The ball is always threatening to fall down the chute, out of play, forgotten and lost. It is harder for people with weak working memories to keep ideas afloat, avoid distractions, and follow through.

Visual thinking addresses these deficits for struggling learners— and gifted ones too—by adding hooks for the recognition networks, process for the strategic networks, and a successful way to work and persevere. The net effect of visual thinking is to provide learners with extra bumpers and flippers to enhance their mental pinball machine. Ideas will ring out like bells, the bright lights of insight will flash, and learning and achieving will become much easier.

This chapter laid the theoretical groundwork for visual thinking. In the next chapter, we take a more personal look at learners and see how visual inquiry addresses the three neural networks and supporting learning theories. We will see how it provides students with better ways to recall information, develop schemas, and express their thinking authentically and meaningfully, and we'll see how it bolsters the strategic networks by reducing cognitive load and expanding working memory. By providing students with an individualized, visual approach to problem solving, these strategies themselves build academic success; with each passing experience, they construct a schema of academic and intellectual perseverance.

CHAPTER 3

Visually Oriented Learners

I am a visually oriented learner. You are too. So are your students. To some degree, we all are—even the vision impaired! In a 2014 NPR interview, Judy Dixon (herself visually impaired), of the Library of Congress's National Library Service for the Blind and Physically Handicapped, was asked about the future of Braille. Her response gets directly to the core of visual learning:

> It's hard to imagine what will come along that could replace Braille for us. Audio is a linear experience—the words come, they go. But with Braille, I can see the word, I can see how it's spelled, I can see how the punctuation is. I don't have to wonder if a word has one *t* or two *t*'s. It just is something I observe when I read a Braille word under my fingers....
>
> I personally am kind of a visual learner—I don't take things in well [with] audio. If I see it in Braille, I remember it, because it goes into my visual memory.[1]

As Dixon reveals, visual learning is not really about vision or the eyes. It is a term used to describe a fundamental human approach to learning that involves perception, imagination, and intuition. Braille, which involves touch, not sight, creates a picture in her mind's eye. The raised bumps of the Braille reader she uses create a touch sensation that she "sees" as images. These "pictures" form her lasting memories of words. In contrast, Dixon describes the auditory process of listening to text as a linear experience in which the words she hears pass in and out of her ears. Despite being visually impaired, she acquires knowledge not from sounds, but from the pictures that linger in her visual memory.

Dixon is not alone. Her experience of learning applies to sighted people as well. According to research conducted by Linda Silverman, director of the Gifted Development Center in Denver, Colorado, approximately 33 percent of students in the regular classroom identified themselves as strongly visual-spatial learners, and well over half of the students identified themselves as "visual-spatial" to some degree.[2] Regrettably, not a lot of classroom teaching is designed to leverage key aspects of the visual nature of learning (such as big-picture thinking and abstract reasoning) for tasks that are not generally considered to be visual—such as writing and taking notes—which is precisely the problem we are addressing in this book.

The gulf between traditional teaching approaches and how contemporary students learn is a growing problem in US schools because, in fact, students with diverse learning needs comprise the majority of students in the classroom. Therefore, teaching with traditional methods is, in effect, teaching to the minority. This may seem counterintuitive at first, but it makes a lot of sense. Inclusive classrooms today are characterized by large numbers of students who are gifted, have diagnosed and undiagnosed learning disabilities, ADHD, dyslexia, and autism spectrum disorders, in addition to English-language learners, indigenous students, and students who are at-risk for other reasons. These nontraditional learners benefit the most from information presented in diverse modalities.

Finally, what should clearly tip the balance toward change is the ubiquitousness of technology. In our digital device–driven world, students are constantly engaged in fast-twitch, trial-and-error methods of learning that are highly visual, highly experimental, and interactive. These forms of technology, which keep us constantly connected, have shifted some of the focus away from activities like writing and note-taking the old-fashioned way. If we aren't using the new, everyday tools of life in the classroom to teach, we aren't preparing our kids for the world they live in. The fact that kids are never more than a click away from a collaborative, interactive experience has made the entire population more visual-spatial and significantly more nonlinear. This combination of new technology and demographic reality requires that we embrace new ways to teach.

The Debate Over Learning Styles and Hemisphere Preference

There is active academic debate about the validity of the concept of "learning styles." Research-based justification for using specific strategies geared toward specific learning preferences (that may align better with how the left or right hemisphere processes information) is not well established and is disputed by some. This dispute stems in part from the challenge of measuring critical thinking, and in part from the difficulty in proving empirical cause-and-effect relationships between teaching practice and learning outcomes. The debate also stems from ambiguity in the definition of what a learning style is, and how it affects people's lives. Regardless of what educational researchers debate, however, many people continue to identify themselves as "visual learners." These millions of individuals are not basing their judgment on a scientific evaluation; rather, they are naming a personal feeling about the way they tend to approach learning. The term may have an informality and a pop-psychology element to it, but it is not without value or merit.

Over time, the term *visual learner*, or *visual-spatial learner*, has evolved to describe one of the two archetypal human learning styles. For many years these learners were labeled "right-brain dominant." In academic circles, the terms "visual learner" and more generally "hemisphere dominance" have become outmoded because they do not adequately reflect the complexity of learning. Visual learning is also not an entirely accurate term because, as Judy Dixon shared, it does not necessarily even involve vision.

While educational research has moved past this oversimplification, the idea of the visually oriented learner remains highly useful in drawing some broad distinctions about how a significant percentage of the world's population tends to process information and approach problem solving. In doing so, it draws attention to the need for learning strategies that benefit all learners.

> The two archetypal learning profiles provide valuable insights that should influence and inform teaching and learning.

The opposite of the **visual-spatial learner** is the **auditory-sequential learner**. Stereotypically scholastically high-achieving, organized, punctual, and linear-thinking, auditory-sequential learners have been dubbed "left-brain-dominant" learners. Along with the concept of learning styles, the idea of hemisphere dominance has been challenged in academic research because it oversimplifies the complex parallel processing and bilateral interaction that occur through the corpus callosum, a thick band of neural tissue that connects the two hemispheres.

Distorted interpretations and simplistic labels make it sound as though we could lop off half our brain and be just fine, as long as it happened to our "nondominant" hemisphere. Most researchers and psychologists have moved beyond the term "hemispheric dominance" because so many factors and exceptions influence how the mind processes information.

Lessons Learned from Brain Hemisphere Research

Learning does not happen only on one side of the mind. Instead, it is complex and individualistic, and it involves complex bilateral interaction throughout the whole brain. The pendulum's swing back from a view of "hemispheric dominance" to a more nuanced whole-brain view builds on the lessons learned from the study of the differences in the way the hemispheres process information. The two archetypal learning profiles provide valuable insights that should influence and inform teaching and learning.

Below is a table summarizing some of the vocabulary that has been used to refer to hemispheric-based learning.

Left-Hemispheric Labels	Right-Hemispheric Labels
Auditory-sequential learner	Visual-spatial learner
Auditory learner	Visual learner
Sequential learner	Spatial learner
Convergent thinker	Divergent thinker
Vertical thinker	Lateral thinker
Linear thinker	Nonlinear thinker

Psychologist J. P. Guilford introduced the terms **divergent thinking** and **convergent thinking** in 1967. Divergent thinking describes the process of generating a lot of possibilities or solutions to a given question or problem. **Convergent thinking**, its opposite, relates to pulling in the necessary information and resources to solve a specific problem or answer a particular question.[3] Convergent thinking has been the domain of scholastic education for generations, and it is easily measured through testing.

The chocolate cake graphic represents convergent thinking (fig. 3.1). If the question is "what do you need to make a chocolate cake?" then the right answer includes specific ingredients. Teaching content that can be answered with certainty and accuracy is the kind of instruction that has been emphasized in classrooms across the United States for decades.

Divergent thinking is different and requires a different approach to problem solving. Divergent and **lateral thinking** refer to creative processes that explore possibilities. Lateral thinking is a term coined by Edward de Bono, author of *Six Thinking Hats*. He articulates a strategy for effective collaborative thinking, planning, and problem solving. This approach facilitates one's ability to thoughtfully consider, listen, share, and reveal all possible aspects of an idea by approaching a question from different points of view.[4]

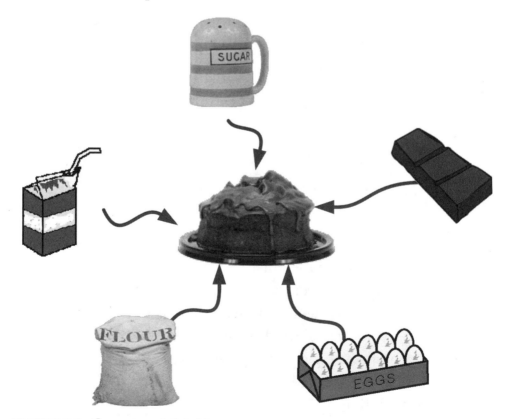

FIGURE 3.1. Convergent thinking.

In an example of divergent, or lateral thinking, one might ask a group how they could make a chocolate cake if they didn't have the right ingredients or even a stove. Answering this question would require participants to understand the purpose of each ingredient in the recipe and the rationale for the procedure so that they could design effective alternatives. This type of thinking is challenging to measure because it elicits many correct responses and the merit of any response is more dependent on the rationale and evidence than the specific answer. Another example of divergent thinking is asking students what kind of dessert would be best for a very important guest. This open-ended question requires prediction, empathy, and creativity. It may lead students to consider the culture of the guest, diet restrictions, the cost of the dessert, and the time it would take to make it; the rudimentary idea could be mapped like figure 3.2. A way to elicit divergent thinking is to ask open-ended questions. The answers are harder to assess, as they do not always conform to a teacher's expected responses, but divergent thinking is critical in innovation and creativity, and it is necessary to teach and practice.

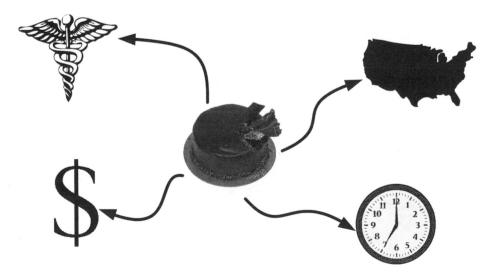

FIGURE 3.2. Divergent thinking.

While research may not prescribe how hemisphere dominance and learning styles should impact education in practice, there is a large body of research that defines the broad characteristics and general domains of the left and right hemispheres. The right brain is the hemisphere that perceives the whole problem and seems less rooted in logic, more oriented toward divergent thinking. Visual-spatial learners may be highly intelligent and appropriately classified as gifted, but they often do not thrive in school or they show inconsistency and imbalance in their academic performance. They are characteristically a sensitive and creative group of whole-to-part, divergent thinkers who tend to see the big picture and may miss details. As a teacher, you may have to wait for this group to get to class because they tend to run late. Often these learners can see an answer to a question but are unable to give you the reasons or steps. Sometimes they actually get worse at academic tasks with too much practice. Contrary to pervasive educational practice and even popular belief, *practice can make imperfect*. For right-brain-oriented learners, and especially for gifted ones, overlearning may not lead to mastery, and boredom can lead to disengagement and carelessness. Overlearning strategies, which do help some at-risk learners, run the risk of reducing academic experiences to rote memorization. Silverman calls this the "killer effect of drill and practice."[5] Naturally divergent thinkers engage fully in meaningful learning experiences that challenge them to create, connect ideas, and apply novel thinking in their work with curriculum subject matter. Often they need to devise their own completely individualistic way of learning.

> Contrary to pervasive educational practice and even popular belief, practice can make *imperfect*.

David Cole, co-author of the inspirational, highly practical book *Learning Outside the Lines*, described his unique approach to writing, which involved creating a 3-D metal sculpture that required welding and soldering. How does that turn into an essay? For Cole, it was the only way![6] For me, and I hope for you and your students, the visual inquiry process described in part 3, which incorporates convergent and divergent thinking, offers a solution.

As Judy Dixon suggested, visual-spatial learning has little to do with vision, and auditory-sequential learning has little to do with hearing. Hemispheric preference does, however, relate to the way an individual will approach a problem and make sense of the world. Neurologists, psychologists, and educators have studied this topic, and the two hemispheres have unique approaches to processing information that both differ from and complement one another. To avoid the trap of trying to design teaching to meet the needs of one part of the brain or the other, we must keep front and center the understanding that:

- People seamlessly use both hemispheres of their brains to think, process information, and learn.
- Strategies that integrate both left-brain and right-brain strengths are best for learning.
- Visual-spatial learners benefit from strategies that help them structure and organize their divergent thinking.
- Auditory-sequential learners benefit from strategies that help them to think divergently.

The table that follows is adapted from *Upside-Down Brilliance* by Linda Silverman and shows the general characteristics of learners who identify themselves as visual-spatial or auditory-sequential.[7]

Auditory-sequential learners are:	Visual-spatial learners are:
Generally strong academic students	Creative types
Comfortable with the right answer	Likely to find novel solutions or to arrive at solutions intuitively
Focused and responsible	Daydreamers

Auditory-sequential learners are:	Visual-spatial learners are:
Academically talented	Creatively, technologically, mechanically, or emotionally gifted
Sensitive to time and deadlines	Seemingly oblivious to the passing of time
Attentive to details	Good at seeing the big picture, but may miss details
Able to progress sequentially from easy to difficult materials	Often bored with easy material, but may tune in with complex or conceptual material
Well-organized	Apt to create unique and personal methods of organization
Able to follow and remember oral directions well	Likely to forget auditory directions quickly
Adept at learning language through drill and practice	Good at mastering language through immersion
Step-by-step learners	Whole-to-part learners
Good at recalling information quickly and accurately	Likely to learn best when they can see relationships
Driven by a sense of responsibility to complete tasks	Motivated by an emotional connection to a teacher or content

These traits provide a set of guidelines for understanding which side of the brain tends to grab the steering wheel and drive when a learner needs to figure something out. The strategies in this book are designed to leverage the strengths of both hemispheres, because we use both in every task we do. Take, for example, a student who has a vision for a recycling project that will reduce waste at her school. This student may feel the importance of the effort, recognize the value to the school and global community, and be able to motivate others with her dream. However, this same individual may struggle or fail to bring the project to fruition if she can't break down the steps, plan, organize, and deliver the details that are required to make it a reality. In contrast, a more linear-thinking individual could devise the perfect plan and arrange the logistics, yet fail to emotionally engage the community in the cause. Motivation, inspiration, and higher purpose find a home in the more sensitive right hemisphere.

This same type of dichotomy holds true for writing a good essay. For instance, the right-brain learner may clearly see that *To Kill a Mockingbird* is about race, prejudice, fear, and loss of innocence. That reader may feel passionately about these themes and become outraged at the injustices perpetrated in the novel. However, when it comes time to write a paper on these subjects, that same reader may fail to articulate those thoughts persuasively unless she can organize them logically and sustain the required working memory. In contrast, an auditory-sequential learner may be able to construct a logically structured paper while failing to capture the emotional impact of the story and the appropriate call to action.

All learners need strategies that get them to their personal finish line. Auditory-sequential learners benefit from gaining a big-picture vision that can guide the steps they naturally follow. Visual-spatial learners benefit from a strategy that breaks down the vision into steps that they can follow. The strategies we explore in part 3 do just that—they support the needs of both visual and auditory learners by harnessing the strengths of the whole brain.

Teaching Visual-Spatial Learners

Think over your teaching experience. Have you ever taught a student who seemed to understand more than she could demonstrate or explain or one who couldn't learn the material your way but somehow found a way to teach herself? These are hallmarks of nonlinear thinkers who see the big picture but don't focus on the details. A visual-spatial chef, for example, will look at the contents of the refrigerator and get a vision for a meal. This chef may draw inspiration from recipes, but will not feel bound to follow the steps.

Teachers of visual-spatial learners can expect to be both elated and frustrated by this group because these kids will come up with incredible insights, yet repeatedly fail to master the basics. Many exhibit characteristics associated with (or they may be diagnosed with) ADHD, dyslexia, or executive-function deficits. Many are gifted. Some strongly visually oriented learners may fall on the autism spectrum. As an educator, I do not focus on these labels. Rather than thinking of these characteristics as conditions, I think of them as the spices that flavor a person's way of functioning in the world. Learning strategies that benefit this population benefit all learners, so, to a degree, what do the labels really accomplish?

Richard Selznick, in his work *The Shut-Down Learner*, avoids the pitfalls and stigma of diagnosis and labeling by looking instead at the impact of underachievement and frustration in school. What learners may "have" is largely irrelevant since they struggle in school, are at risk of failing, and find the whole experience oppressive. Selznick calls these kids "shut-down learners." Many of these students experience difficulties in traditional school settings that measure student achievement through narrowly defined "correct" responses, attentive behavior, and an ability to follow auditory directions. These measurements emphasize successful convergent thinking. Highly prized is a student's capacity to answer questions quickly and complete tasks in a direct manner. These assessments do not measure the strengths of visual learners—only their weaknesses.[8]

In many cases, such students struggle with academic tasks like organization, writing, and recall, but when they are curious, they immerse themselves and are actually highly driven learners. As noted by Selznick:

> Shut-Down Learners readily perceive patterns. They can visualize things well. Most of their thought process is dominated by visualization, as opposed to thinking through language....

When these children are engaged in tasks that require spatial aptitude, they rarely exhibited distractibility, hyperactivity, or restlessness. These children can engage in hands-on tasks for hours.[9]

Visual-spatial-oriented learners often discount their own intellectual strengths because the areas in which they excel have typically not been prized in school. Selznick calls these students "Lego-kids" because they tend to thrive at making things, finding creative and novel solutions, thinking intuitively, and teaching themselves new material in unpredictable ways. Only recently have these intellectual qualities gained traction as essential areas to develop. For generations, the scholastic emphasis on timed tests, rapid recall, and correct responses has taken a toll on self-esteem. Luckily, in the twenty-first century, many of the strengths of the visual learner are emerging as essential drivers for innovation and success.

> Visual-spatial-oriented learners often discount their own intellectual strengths because the areas in which they excel have typically not been prized in school.

Even bastions of fact-and-recall instruction such as medical schools are acknowledging the benefits of teaching holistically—a departure from the approach that has dominated for fifty years. New studies are showing that medical schools that emphasize empathy, observation, listening, and creativity produce doctors who are more accurate in their diagnoses and have lower burnout rates.[10]

Divergent thinkers are a group with unique gifts, but many face profound challenges because completing tasks and even executing the steps to reach their own goals requires them to reel in their creativity and follow through. For those who essentially need to teach themselves, learning and accomplishing goals can be like reinventing the wheel with each new task. It is easy to understand why these students excel in hands-on projects. They intuitively see how things fit together. However, to be successful with intellectual and analytical activities such as writing papers and comparing and contrasting ideas, they need something different. These learners particularly benefit from strategies that allow them to work with all parts of an idea, like a puzzle, and find a solution to that puzzle in their own way. The solution I am proposing augments divergent and convergent thinking by allowing learners to explore a concept in their own way, but with the tools to organize that idea into a clear and cohesive representation that can be used to complete traditional assignments.

Working Memory and Executive-Function Problems

Working memory and executive function play critical roles in an individual's ability to hone an idea. It is hard work for any student to organize ideas and integrate new knowledge, but for one with deficits in these areas, the amount of mental juggling required to manage, maintain, and assimilate information can exceed the student's working memory capacity. These students can, however, strengthen their strategic networks by using methods that stretch their working memory and therefore improve executive function.

When our executive function and working memory are working well, they allow us to integrate information so we can construct meaning and act appropriately with that understanding. People with frontal lobe injuries or numerous learning disabilities suffer in diverse ways because of improper functioning of the strategic networks and weak working memories. While research on the root causes of ADHD is ongoing, various studies have looked at the role of blood flow in the

frontal lobe, the function of neurotransmitters in the brain, hered-
ity, and injury. In all of these cases, the manifestation is weak executive function, characterized by impulsivity and distractibility, as well
as poor organization, time management, and planning. The research
of Helena Westerberg shows that children with ADHD have weaker
working memories than those in the control group of her study.[11] Her
work empirically demonstrates a long-known fact about individuals with ADHD: they tend to be more forgetful, they struggle to follow directions and maintain a train of thought, and they fidget and act
impulsively more often than their peers.

These symptoms are accurate, but they do not describe what it *feels*
like to be a person who has ADHD, which I want to relate by adding a
personal account. At many points throughout the day, a person with
ADHD will experience a deluge of ideas that come crashing into his
mind like waves, accompanied by an exhilarating and heightened
feeling of alertness. I believe that some of the excessive energy that a
person with ADHD exhibits comes from the sheer exuberance he feels
from this rush. Ideas arrive fast and furious; however, they are often
incomplete. The learner perceives glimmers and flashes but has no
time to fit them together or sort them out. Before he can get a handle
on one, another crashes in. I think many people with ADHD blurt out
thoughts impulsively because saying them out loud helps them linger.
They need to interrupt because they know that their idea isn't going
to stick around until the teacher calls on them. Often, the idea is not
complete when the outburst happens, so the blurt is just that—a half-
baked tangent that comes off as a disruption. As disconnected as these
fragments may seem, however, they often contain creative glimmers,
relevant connections, and even hidden insights that observant, patient
teachers may draw out.

Individuals with autism spectrum disorders suffer from executive-
function deficits in different ways. Many have prodigious memories,
but an inability to integrate and assimilate information effectively.
They frequently have trouble separating what is relevant and important

from what is not. Weak-functioning strategic networks cause these individuals to have difficulty relating to others, acting appropriately, and implementing successful strategies to execute plans. All of the cognitive information they receive becomes a distracting mental static, and they struggle to sort out the noise.[12] Those with pronounced working-memory and executive-function challenges need a strategy for handling their intensely nonlinear thinking and flashes of creativity—so they can create doorways to marvelous breakthroughs rather than traveling a mental labyrinth of dead ends.

Metacognition

One way to find a path through this maze is through **metacognition.** Metacognition is the ability to reflect on our own actions and thoughts as if we were observing ourselves from a position outside our mind looking in. It is the act of "thinking about thinking" and is one of the traits that makes us human. John Flavell, one of the pillars of educational psychology, and foundational researcher of metacognition, describes it as "cognitive monitoring" and the ability to know when one "understands" or "does not understand." In his studies of memory, he asked preschool and elementary school children to study sets of words until they could recall them correctly. The older children fared better, and Flavell explained that older students had a greater recognition of the feeling of *understanding* and recognition of *not understanding* than their younger counterparts.[13]

Metacognitive experiences have a strong affective component. Feelings connected to experiences of understanding and intellectual success are powerful and positive. When a person reads and can visualize the scene in his mind's eye, he knows that he understands the passage. When a learner "gets" the mathematical concept and knows she can solve the problem, she has feelings of success and confidence. Conversely, when a metacognitive learner loses the idea of the passage, he or she recognizes the feeling of confusion and applies a new strategy, such as rereading, looking at prior examples, or asking questions.

For success in school and the workplace, metacognition leads to achievement and innovation. Fortunately, it can be taught! Teaching students to see patterns by diagramming ideas helps them reflect on their thinking and see how to bring those ideas to fruition. Visualizing and mapping strategies provide this insight, helping learners to assess their own understanding.

Implications for Teaching: How the Brain's Networks Operate

Our exploration of the three primary neural networks and learning theories sets the table for what we educators need to do. We have to synthesize what we know about learning into a cohesive strategy that:

- Bolsters recognition using multisensory approaches that activate more parts of the brain
- Helps students have positive learning experiences that make them feel successful and confident, thus fostering perseverance
- Enhances working memory and decreases the cognitive load
- Serves as a metacognitive strategy that helps students self-monitor learning

Visual inquiry provides a set of guiding principles and explicit steps that meets these requirements. It is a benefit for learners of all ages and diverse cognitive abilities. It is also applicable across a broad range of topics. We will break down the alignment of visual inquiry to human cognition by exploring a simple example from work that I conducted with students in a Philadelphia high school. Original student work is not included due to privacy policies, but the following diagram is a composite representative from that experience.

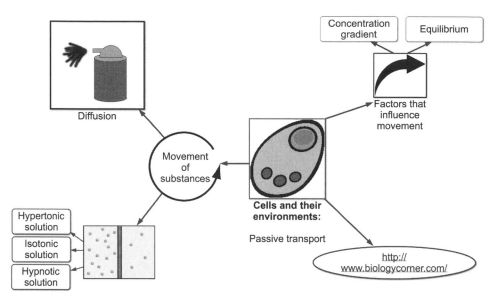

FIGURE 3.3. Passive transport web.

High school science students were asked to create semantic webs to represent the concept of passive transport (fig. 3.3). The student work (and this representative model) was created on a laptop computer using Inspiration Software. Content was taken from the textbook and from several websites. The diagram represents a synthesis of knowledge being learned. It is not a copy of a diagram from a textbook. The example illustrates much of the theory behind visual inquiry and, as will be explained below, helps tie together the concepts introduced thus far.

Recognition Networks

Visual inquiry gave the science students a clear and simple way to represent passive transport. The process of creating the web activated many specialized regions in their recognition networks through the use of image, shape, color, spatial relationships, and text. (Note that the actual diagram uses color, but it is reproduced here in black and white.) As students read about passive transport, they found symbols to represent the ideas they encountered. Images paired with text exemplify dual coding theory. The use of select visual symbols and only a few words decreases the cognitive load necessary to understand a concept. By using images, spatial relationships, and text together, the learner engages both the visual right hemisphere and the sequential left hemisphere, thus doubling the cognitive resources dedicated to learning the vocabulary and understanding passive transport.

> By using image, spatial relationships, and text together, the learner engages both the visual right hemisphere and the sequential left hemisphere, thus doubling cognitive resources dedicated to learning the vocabulary and understanding the components of a concept.

Webbing facilitates recall of prior knowledge and provides the learner with a way to make the concept meaningful. The visual representations add to her schema of the topic. The labels and pictures make it easier to manage all of the new content that needs to be integrated into her final product and ultimately assimilated into long-term memory. The combination of image, text, and spatial relationships provides a multisensory coding of this information, which decreases the cognitive load and eases the working memory needed to learn the concept.

Affective Networks

The affective networks play a significant role in the way students create meaning in their webs. Color, image, and the spacing of symbols are all individual choices based on personal and aesthetic preferences. In this example, did the students choose spray paint to represent "diffusion" because of a connection to that object? Perhaps some urban art seen daily on a walk to school served as a reminder to reinforce the concept of diffusion? The personal choices behind the depiction of passive transport create a connection between the students' own experiences and the content, which adds strength to the concept and transitions it into long-term memory.

The successful creation of a visual representation is in itself an affective experience that builds perseverance and self-confidence, which can positively impact future learning. Because our students had success representing passive transport visually, maybe they will have success representing the next science topic visually too. Gradually, the strategy itself becomes a schema that becomes its own building block for learning any new concept.

Strategic Networks

A web is a learning strategy that helps the brain efficiently integrate new knowledge. It does so in a way that taxes the strategic networks to the least degree possible. Learning is complex. To be capable of understanding passive transport, a student needs the executive function to simultaneously remember vocabulary (like osmosis), understand new concepts (like diffusion), and see the big picture of how those components fit together. The cognitive load required for this task is significant. It requires a strong working memory. We have explained how dual coding helps recognition and how the affective networks add personal meaning by adding hooks into the idea related to feelings and experience. Both of these types of activity decrease cognitive load and therefore assist the strategic networks in assimilating the knowledge.

As a strategy, visual inquiry offers many tools that facilitate learning. First and foremost, it gives the learner a framework to visualize a concept as a **spatial arrangement.** The student visually organizes the content diagrammatically in a way that has meaning, with a central main idea and details that radiate outward. This spatial relationship is critical. By creating a hierarchy of information that begins with a main topic and spreads out from there, the learner is able to structure content so that items with equal conceptual weight have an equal visual weight. This visual arrangement allows students to show relationships graphically without losing any critical content. In our passive transport web example, the relationship between "osmosis" and "diffusion" is clear to anyone viewing the work. The students' sources are also clearly conveyed by a specific shape and text. The organization of the web creates a visual grammar with an inherent logic that our minds can process and understand. Webs possess a visual literacy.

Learning with Our Natural Gifts

Throughout human evolution, we have used all of our cognitive assets as a universal toolkit for finding patterns and solving problems. Originally, this strategy was essential for survival. Now it is essential for innovation. We know the most effective approaches to learning involve a multi-sensory experience that engages many parts of the brain. We understand that specialized nodes interpret and route that information, which moves through the brain. We also know that broad neural networks function together seamlessly to give meaning to perception and to integrate new knowledge.

The process of visual inquiry takes us back to our innate strengths as learners. Pictures and text depicted through spatial relationships together provide hooks that augment working memory, allowing learners to work with increasingly complex topics. Visual inquiry engages the whole mind with a framework that neither constricts by rigid order nor muddles with unbridled creativity. Visual inquiry allows thoughts to bounce around the mind—like they do as they travel through the neural networks—and yet be structured by a set of rules that harnesses them constructively.

The nonlinear but interconnected flow of information through the brain from neuron to neuron and through neural networks matches our method of visual inquiry and enhances learning for everyone. It is no coincidence that this unique approach to learning truly does match the way we naturally think.

Visually oriented learners are not rare or unique, even though they might feel that way. They can thrive academically, though they may need more freedom to explore ideas than a traditional didactic teaching model affords. In our knowledge-based society, where the novel and new, the repurposed and mashed up, are at the epicenter of opportunity, our original, nonconforming, creative types may feel like oddballs, but they have an edge. To see more of them blossom, however, we first need to help them get through school intellectually confident and emotionally intact. To ensure that happens, we educators need to create an environment where they can thrive, and give them the tools to learn, create, and complete what they dream.

PART 2

Putting Visual Inquiry into Practice

Thinking visually is natural—we do it all the time. Using visual inquiry as a first approach to tackle a learning challenge, however, is a leap; in fact, it is the Visual Leap. You need to trust that mapping and drawing ideas is not child's play—it is a serious and efficient way to access the full potential of the human mind. It can transform how you learn, how you teach, and how you teach others how to learn for themselves. The trust required to make this leap is significant. Learning this way can feel different than it ever has before—even if the new feeling is one of success and ease. There may not be many other people you know who teach, learn, take notes, or capture group conversations this way.

Because visual thinking gets an idea out of your head and into a format that can be worked with, its applications are limitless. Police officers use visual inquiry in complex cases by posting pictures on bulletin boards and pinning up coded and colored notes, which they can move around and revise as the case develops. This technique helps them see all of the information at once. Architects use a process called bubble mapping when they plan projects. Collaborative thinking by corporate and academic teams benefits from a visual language that everyone shares. The remainder of this book brings the principles of visual thinking into practices that can be applied in classrooms, used by individuals, and used for academic and professional tasks like reading, writing, speaking, and listening. Chapter 4 introduces the power of webbing and demonstrates that thinking is fundamentally nonlinear. Chapter 5 explores the laws of visual thinking that guide how we apply these strategies, and chapter 6 delivers the step-by-step process for visual inquiry and explains how to teach it to others.

CHAPTER 4

Introducing Webbing

In the summer between her tenth and eleventh grade years, a student named Marguerite enrolled in my visual learning program. After a few sessions, I did a little test with the group. I asked students to take ten minutes and write a quick summary of their weekends. (The following writing samples and web are unedited.) These are the forty-three words Marguerite produced:

> On Friday I went to my cousin's birthday party. That night, some girls from Pennsylvania came to my house. The next day all of us went to the 4H Fair. Today, we had the first meeting of our youth group. It was a fun weekend.

Then I asked students to create a web to plan their ideas, after which I instructed them to write for another ten minutes. Here is the web Marguerite produced:

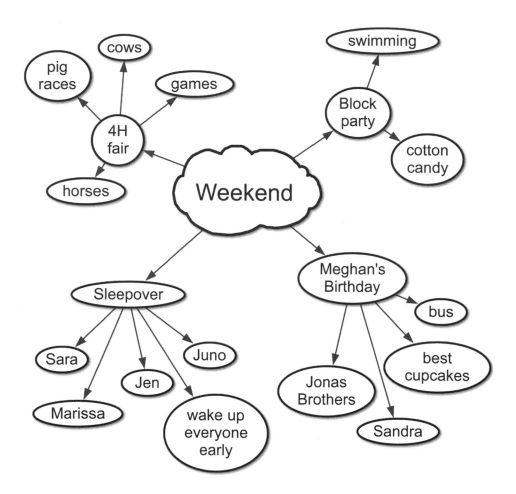

FIGURE 4.1. Student web of her weekend.

After her web was complete, she used ten minutes to write the follow-ing response, which is unedited except for name changes:

Thursday night I went to the Jonas Brothers concert with my cousin Jamie and our friends Sandra and Meghan. The next day was her birthday so, she had a birthday party. Our cousin Marissa came and I don't usually get to see her so it was fun being with her. Also, my friend Trish was there too. Jamie had the best cupcakes at her birthday; they were from Coldstone Creamery, my favorite ice cream place! That night, after Jamie's birthday party, when I came home the people from Pennsylvania had arrived at my house. We had four of them sleeping over our house. The girls slept in my room and I slept in my brother's room. Friday we went to the 4H Fair and there they had horse and pig races, shopping, food and a competition on big cows. That night we decided we wanted to watch a movie. We tried to watch A Walk to Remember, but it wouldn't work for some reason. Instead, we watched Juno. Saturday we were having a block party. We had to wake up early to set up the games and food. The cotton candy was the best! It lasted until one and it was very fun. Later that night we went over to our friend's, the Johnsons' house for a swim party. I took my friends with me and the car ride up was so loud from all of our singing. My mom had a headache by the time we got to the party. For desert we had an ice cream sandwich cake which was delicious. After desert we went back home and got to bed early because we were exhausted from all our swimming and singing. Sunday we went to church and just relaxed all day. This morning we had to wake up very early to help get ready for youth group. I was teaching the preschoolers and kindergarteners with help from Sandra and Meghan. We had so many little kids running around! But, it was so much fun. After we left I went home and got ready for tutoring, and that's where I am now.

This real-life example shocked me as much as it shocked Marguerite. In her first go-round, she looked as bored writing her summary as I was reading it. In the second writing phase, by contrast, Marguerite lost herself in the process. Not only did she write more than eight times as much, but she was also joyous while doing it, reliving the highlights of the weekend. Her sentences are full of rich storytelling, humor, and vivid detail. Incidentally, her work was not an exception. Almost every child in that class had a similarly dramatic result.

Part of this transformation can likely be attributed to the teaching method. Marguerite did the first trial cold. Before the second trial, she did a prewriting activity that activated her memory and helped her organize her thoughts. The profound effect of the webbing as a prewriting activity, however, is worth a close look. It appeared to break down barriers to writing in Marguerite's mind and allowed an outpouring of information to cascade onto the page. Her inhibitions fell away as her thoughts spilled out. Any concerns about grammar or spelling or even sentence structure evaporated as her ideas took center stage.

For Marguerite, webbing was the mother of all prewriting strategies. The process did everything cognitive science prescribes for learning in terms of accessing prior knowledge and having an affective connection to the content. It also provided a structure to decrease cognitive load by giving her a way to capture ideas as they cropped up, regardless of where they would end up in the final product. If you read the passage again, however, perhaps you will agree that once she got the idea into a workable format, something magical happened; the science of learning united with the art of creation. Marguerite forgot herself, and the result was a beautiful original statement. The process that Marguerite engaged in was so successful because it combined divergent thinking, which she used to freely recall the full scope of her idea, with convergent thinking, which helped refine that thinking into a cohesive structure.

> The webbing process did everything cognitive science prescribes for learning in terms of accessing prior knowledge and having an affective connection to the content. It also provided a structure to decrease cognitive load by giving the student a way to capture ideas as they cropped up.

Ideas rarely develop in a sequential, linear form, yet they must be organized that way to be effective. Just think about a clear argument versus a muddled argument—one is persuasive and one is dismissed. The normal way of thinking blends both convergent and divergent thinking. With conversations, whether academic or social, the same is true. Topics, details, and examples are introduced in an unpredictable order. Sometimes ideas develop sequentially as they build logically. At other times ideas bounce around, triggered by associations that take the ideas in new directions. Sometimes a statement will generate a seemingly unrelated new idea. Conversation is an example of a nonlinear process with which we all have experience, but ideas that we explore in our minds evolve the same way.

Because few people naturally develop ideas in a linear fashion from A→Z, there is a tremendous need for a learning strategy that can transform nonlinear thinking into an organized idea. Webbing does this by incorporating the strengths of both the left and right hemispheres, giving the learner a way to catch ideas as they fly around and then piece them together to create clear concepts. The visual anatomy of the web makes this possible.

Visual Anatomy of the Semantic Web

Semantic webs have an anatomy that contributes to their versatility and logic. Figure 4.2 is an image of a web. It is made up of nodes, or symbols (which can be represented with shapes and images), and connections, or links (which can be drawn or computer-generated). These connections are often, though not necessarily, depicted as arrows.

A node's level is defined by how many levels away it is from the main idea, which is designated the Level 1 node. Subtopics are Level 2 nodes. Details are at Level 3. The web in Figure 4.2 has Level 4 nodes, which can be considered details of a detail. Depending on the complexity of an idea, webs can branch out infinitely. There is no limit to the number of levels they can have.

An important component of the semantic web—one that helps

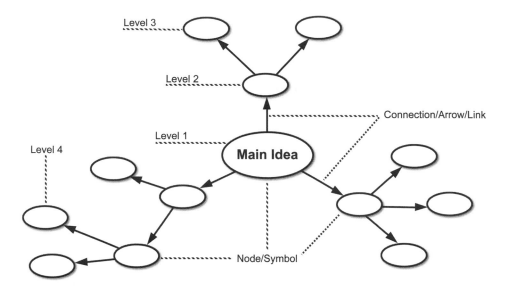

FIGURE 4.2. Anatomy of a web.

executive function—is its ability to reduce the amount of written text needed to express an idea. For emerging readers or people who struggle with text, the implications for reading comprehension, note taking, and communication are vast.

Webs, mind maps, and diagrams share an extraordinary characteristic: the text they use is almost entirely made up of nouns. Arrows essentially take the place of verbs. This is a key component of their inherent visual literacy. In webs and maps, most words can drop out without sacrificing meaning. In fact, their meaning is enhanced by the use of fewer words. Webs are virtually devoid of adjectives and adverbs. There are almost no interjections or conjunctions. Pronouns are rare because the noun is used instead. In short, a web essentially omits eight of the nine parts of speech. Virtually the only necessary text remaining is nouns! These can often be represented with pictures or words. The impact of this linguistic simplification for helping learners to organize ideas and reflect on their learning cannot be understated. Mind maps and webs often reduce the words needed to communicate an idea by 80 percent.

This reduction is remarkable because it reflects a fascinating inverse relationship with the work of speech therapists in their efforts to teach early language to nonverbal individuals. Speech therapists divide language into **fringe words** and **core words**. Fringe words occur with low frequency and have specific meaning. "Table," "skateboard," and "bus" are examples of fringe words. Speech therapists often use pictures to teach these words, and they are also the kinds of words that are necessary in mind maps and webs to show meaning visually. Core words are essential to verbal and written communication because they are the glue that holds together the meaning. Examples of core words are "over," "on," "I," "help," "mine," "where," and "in." Imagine oral communication without them! Eighty percent of the words in our written or oral communication are core words, leaving just 20 percent for fringe words. This amazing fact explains why mind maps and webs can so easily communicate an idea visually with only 20 percent of the words of traditional text.[1] Webs require only fringe words because their visual structure communicates the rest. (For more information about core words and fringe words, visit aaclanguagelab.com.)

Visual inquiry is at heart a metacognitive strategy. When students can represent an idea visually, their understanding is evident. If the diagram makes sense, the idea makes sense. A learner cannot successfully fake a diagram. A teacher would see it instantly. More importantly, visual inquiry helps the learner to recognize when he is confused because the diagram reveals any gaps in structure, content, and logic. Done well, it provides an elegant skeletal representation of an idea. By eliminating the core words, the mind can freely and quickly depict thoughts without getting bogged down with artifacts of language that are critical for verbal or written communication, but not for thinking. This simple and transformative dynamic is the "special sauce" for visual thinking because fringe words give learners a way to capture the essential parts of their ideas before they forget them. The simplicity of the web's anatomy makes this possible. It allows individuals (and groups of people working together) to follow the unpredictable course of naturally occurring divergent thinking and turn that flow of creativity into actionable knowledge.

Proof of Nonlinear Thinking

The concept of nonlinear, divergent thinking is abstract, yet it is easily shown with a real-life example. The following proof demonstrates that constructing an idea is a nonlinear process. It also shows that, through visual inquiry, webbing harnesses divergent thinking while providing the conditions for linear, convergent thinking. The result is a method that naturally uses right-brain and left-brain thinking harmoniously to construct a perfectly organized idea.

This example comes from a group conversation that I led in a workshop for teachers. I have done this and similar activities hundreds of times. This particular activity lasted for ten to fifteen minutes. To execute it, I projected my computer onto a large screen, and I used Inspiration Software to capture the information. I was the scribe and facilitator, writing down what was said in real time.

The objectives for this activity were:

1. To get everyone actively involved and participating in the workshop
2. To glean teachers' needs in order to personalize the workshop
3. To model the process of webbing and visual inquiry

Step 1. I posed the question: "What do your students struggle with academically?" This is what teachers saw projected:

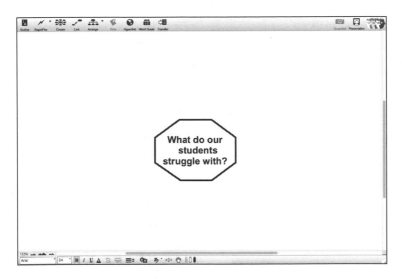

FIGURE 4.3. Step 1 of proof of nonlinear thinking.

The question "What do our students struggle with?" is the main idea. It is the Level 1 node of the web.

Step 2. I gathered responses to the question from participants. The first answer called out was "decoding," so I put that on the screen.

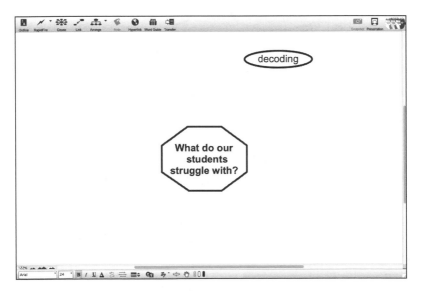

FIGURE 4.4. Step 2 of proof of nonlinear thinking. The first idea is "decoding."

As there were no links at this point in the exercise, it was not clear what level the "decoding" node would possess at the culmination of the activity. After a few minutes, many teachers had responded and I placed their answers on the screen. The brainstorm had become populated with ideas. Now the screen looked like this:

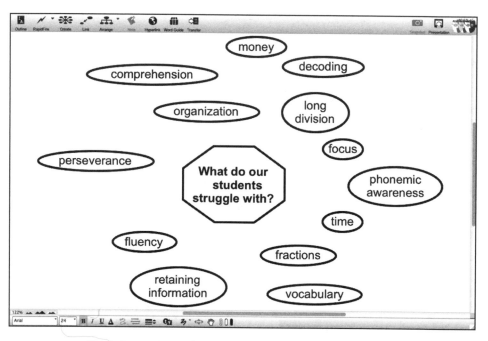

FIGURE 4.5. Step 2 continued: gathering the group's ideas.

Step 3. I asked participants to group their ideas. As teachers called out the items that belonged together, I dragged the unlinked, floating nodes into piles as directed by the group, and an organization began to emerge.

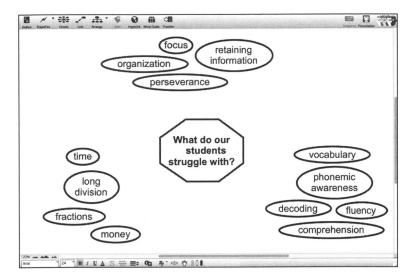

FIGURE 4.6. Step 3 of the proof of nonlinear thinking: grouping ideas.

Step 4. In this step, I prompted the teachers to identify categories for those details. I added these new ideas to the map and placed them between the groups and the Level 1 main topic.

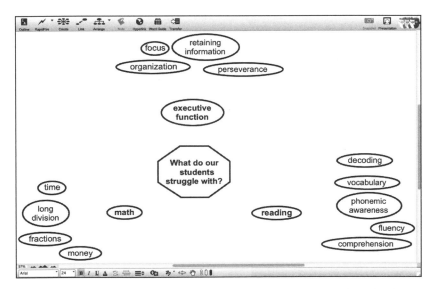

FIGURE 4.7. Step 4 of the proof of nonlinear thinking: adding subtopics to the map.

When teachers reconsidered the details of their ideas in the context of the subtopics, they added more items and moved items around.

Step 5. In the next phase, we used the software to link ideas. This led to the fully connected web, which represents the group's collective response to the initial question. In the prior phases of this process, all nodes were unconnected, and thus were "floating nodes," a term we will refer to throughout the book. Once linked, these nodes assume a level in the hierarchy of the idea, as per figure 4.2, which explains the anatomy of the web.

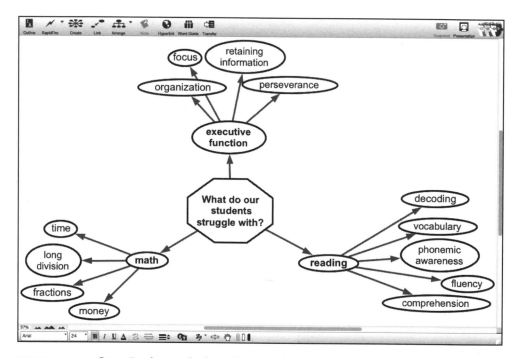

FIGURE 4.8. Step 5 of proof of nonlinear thinking: linking ideas.

Step 6. In this final step, to enhance the meaning, we used the software to add some symbolic representation to the web. Most mind-mapping software tools do this, and even in hand-drawn maps, it is advisable to draw imagery that emphasizes the concept being developed.

Because this example was intended to prove that thinking is naturally a nonlinear process, I also changed the first idea that was added to
the web in Step 2.

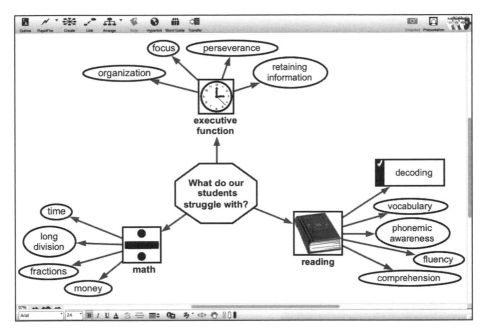

FIGURE 4.9. Step 6 of proof of nonlinear thinking: symbolic representation.

As you can see, the group enhanced the content by selecting images
to represent the subtopics: a clock for executive function, a book for
reading, and a division sign for math.

You may also notice that I changed the symbol for "decoding." I did
this to indicate it was the first response to the original question. Notice
where it ended up on the web: as a Level 3 node, which makes it a detail.
If ideas were linear, the first answer offered would have been one of the
subtopics: executive function, reading, or math. But it wasn't. We do not
naturally think in a linear manner, though we need ideas to be linear in
order to communicate them clearly.

Analysis

The process of webbing this conversation using this specific method reveals several critical points that have a profound impact on teaching and learning.

1. Ideas do not develop in a linear fashion, and in fact, an idea may develop from any point of entry.
2. Webbing engages both sides of the brain in divergent and convergent thinking.
3. The process allows all learners to engage with the ideas in ways they find intuitive.
4. The process provides a format for critical thinking and active listening.
5. This process is easy for teachers to do in class.

This dynamic exercise actively engaged a large group, as well as the whole mind of all of the participants. It began by eliciting recall (lower-order thinking) and culminated with analysis (higher-order thinking). The grouping decisions forced participants to think critically, as the process of defining categories is rarely clear-cut. This process invited debate and thoughtful evaluation. The fact that participants could see the components of the topic at all times helped to manage the cognitive load needed to grapple with the ideas.

The visual depiction of this conversation shows that the natural order of thinking is nonlinear. Our topic began with a main topic, but from there it followed its own course. As we have seen, the first contribution, "decoding," ended up as a Level 3 detail deep down in the web. The process seamlessly captured the conversation in real time. Ideas were added in a divergent thinking process. You can say that this process put the puzzle pieces of the idea onto the table. With the pieces visible for all to see, the conversation took a new turn. Participants began to construct that idea by seeing how it tied together—a powerful example of convergent thinking in action. This method allowed people to generate the ideas creatively, and then apply visual inquiry to analyze and edit them into a highly structured and organized visual representation.

It's very important to understand the order in which hierarchical thinking occurs. Most ideas we work with start with a Level 1 main topic. Our topic for this exercise was "struggling learners." Next, all the participants listened, spoke, and reacted to one another. During this phase we recalled experiences and added them to the visualization. These comprised our Level 3 details. As we began to apply convergent thinking to see how these details fit together, the Level 2 subtopics revealed themselves or were added to the map. Visual inquiry led to a cohesive hierarchical structure to our idea that holds it together and makes a lot of sense. The order of our thinking progressed from "Level 1" to "Level 3" and then culminated with "Level 2."

Therefore, the evolution of an idea is in fact:

Main Topic → Detail → Subtopic
Level 1 → Level 3 → Level 2
Thus proving that organized thinking is as easy as 1–3–2!

However, organized writing, persuasive speaking, and almost all good final-form deliverables—whether they are outlines, essays, proposals, or plans—need to be organized in a traditional order:

Main Topic → Subtopic → Detail
Level 1 → Level 2 → Level 3

This visual inquiry method allows learners to manage the transitions between the nonlinear thinking needed to develop an idea and the linear thinking necessary to do something useful with it. It is the only learning strategy I have ever encountered that captures the constant ebb and flow of divergent and convergent thinking and yields a structured, actionable plan.

> This method of visual thinking is the only strategy that allows learners to manage the transitions between the nonlinear thinking needed to develop an idea and the linear thinking necessary to do something useful with it.

Individuals need to use this method to study and learn because it leverages the whole mind in a uniquely efficient way. For groups, webbing captures the maximum human intellectual capital in the room because all groups contain both those with preferences for right-brain-oriented thinking and those with preferences for sequential thinking. For all of these reasons, and for others that reveal themselves with application and practice, webbing with visual inquiry is the quintessential thinking strategy and the most necessary skill we can teach our students to use.

CHAPTER 5

The Laws of Webbing

Webbing is gloriously simple and highly intuitive. It has few rules, but the ones it does have are black and white. This rare combination of flexibility and formality makes it an easy strategy both to use and to teach to your students. For teachers, webbing may even peel hours off time spent lesson planning. This chapter explores the laws that make webbing so effective in engaging both the left and right hemispheres in the process of visual inquiry. These laws bridge the hemispheres and establish webs and mind maps as visual outlines that correlate precisely to traditional outlines. This duality is the killer app of webbing. It allows learners to think creatively and then to use that creativity to work in a linear fashion. This is the key to maximizing the mind's potential.

Three Simple Laws

The laws of webbing amount to a visual grammar. The rules produce a visual literacy that aligns with the way our minds process information, and their elegant simplicity is critical to their utility. Students find it liberating to have a clear set of guidelines that helps them think critically because webs present information in a way that humans are cognitively designed to handle. As we explore webs in detail, we will delve into their power to harness both convergent and divergent thinking. Following are the three immutable laws of semantic webs.

Students find it liberating to have a clear set of guidelines that helps them think critically, because webs present information in a way that humans are cognitively designed to handle.

Law #1: The main idea goes in the middle.
Law #2: Connections branch out from the center.
Law #3: Connections never close a loop.

The simple semantic web shown in figure 5.1 adheres to all of the laws. Note that (1) the main idea is located in the center, (2) the links that connect the nodes branch out from the center, and (3) the connections never close a loop.

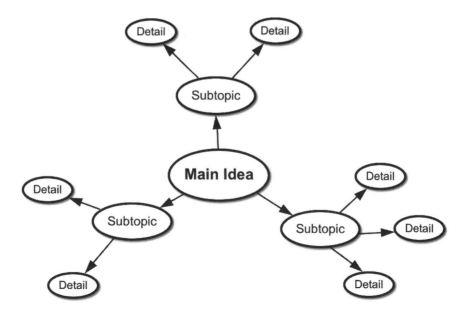

FIGURE 5.1. Semantic web.

Please take a moment to appreciate just how *unremarkable* this graphic organizer is. It is absolutely simple and clear. It is perfectly easy to look at and study. It looks like it could represent just about any idea—because it can!

The simplicity of webs and the comprehension they foster can be deceptive. They can lull those of us in education into forgetting about them because they are so easy to take for granted. And considering the static, graphic-organizer printouts teachers commonly use, this preconception is understandable because only simple ideas can fit into these organizers. In contrast, when webs and maps are hand-drawn or developed with computers, they can grow to represent virtually any idea, giving them an infinitely greater ability to become a flexible method of thinking.

A web's simplicity, however, is precisely what makes it so valuable for learners of all ages, including adults and professionals, to explore ideas of varying levels of complexity. Visualizing information through webbing simplifies thinking and allows learners to make elusive breakthroughs. The laws of webbing explain their visual grammar and substantiate these claims.

Law #1: The Main Idea Goes in the Middle

By definition, the main idea is placed in the middle of a semantic web. This placement may seem mundane, but it is actually quite profound. Centrality of the main idea opens pathways for learning. Our minds naturally "look for" the main topic in the middle of the map. Therefore, by placing it there—rather than at the top—we attract the eye and provide a starting place.

> Centrality of the main idea opens pathways for learning. Our minds naturally "look for" the main topic in the middle of the map.

This visual concept is long-established in artistic composition. The center of a painting is the natural focus. In fact, it is so visually magnetic that contemporary artists go to great lengths to avoid putting objects in the center of a work, to encourage the eye to move around the composition. But webbing is not art, and in this case, it is an asset to place the main topic in the center because it creates a focus to begin to understand the idea.

Conceptually, we are comfortable with the idea that the main topic belongs in the middle because it matches the way we tend to organize our world. People (for the most part) are the centers of their own universe. Just take a moment to think about your life. You are at the center. What are your branches? Family? Work? Hobbies? Friends? Your weekly obligations? Facets of our lives could be visualized in many ways, but one simple way to depict them is in the form of a semantic web.

Our ego-driven worldview is not the only reason we are comfortable with Law #1. Many topics lend themselves to a visual representation that follows this model. The federal government has three branches that can all be clearly shown visually as a web. The solar system can be shown as a web with the sun in the center, as can examples of foreshadowing in a novel. Whether or not you consider yourself a visual learner, it is likely that you have doodled or sketched, without any training or deliberate effort on your part, a representation that has the appearance of a semantic web, complete with a main idea in the middle and arrows branching out. That is to be expected. When we begin to explore a concept, it is logical to locate the highest level in the hierarchy of that idea squarely in the middle.

Law #2: Connections Branch Out from the Center

The direction of the links is essential. Links create the visual literacy of the web and the logic of the idea, replacing many core words, like verbs and prepositions, which would otherwise be necessary to convey ideas clearly. Whether they are hand-drawn or created with software, links establish visual relationships that impart meaning. They also guide your eyes along their path. By providing a direction for the eyes to follow, arrows define the hierarchy of the content. We already defined that a Level 1 idea at the center of the web is the main idea. Level 2 nodes are subtopics of the main idea, and so forth. In mind mapping, these are called **Parent→Child relationships**, and the concept is the same for webs. No matter how far out you build an idea, the law of connections holds true. Arrows always branch outward from the center, with topics always linked from the Parent to the Child.

Always: Level 1 → Level 2 → Level 3 → Level 4
Never: Level 4 → Level 3 → Level 2 → Level 1

This clear structure is a gift. The relationships created by arrows make it easy to see when an idea has parallel construction and when it doesn't. Webs also make it easy to ensure that topics of equal conceptual weight are located at the same level in the web.

Outward branching links are a natural extension of Law #1, in which we identified the main idea as the center of the web and the origin of the arrows. Our eyes naturally understand these Parent→Child relationships and instinctively use the center as a starting place. This point is worth highlighting, because many forms of visual communication begin at the top. Most text-based material works this way, and we have been exhaustively trained both explicitly and through our experiences reading and writing to use the top as a starting point for working with text. But our eyes know better when it comes to webs, and they need no special training. They naturally begin at the center, at the origin of the arrows, and follow the arrows' paths outward to other areas of importance.

This law of visual literacy is profound and absolute. The direction of arrows creates a hierarchical order from largest idea to smallest detail. This creates an intrinsic legibility that can be accurately interpreted by readers and nonreaders alike.

In a clearly conveyed idea, all of the content at the same hierarchical

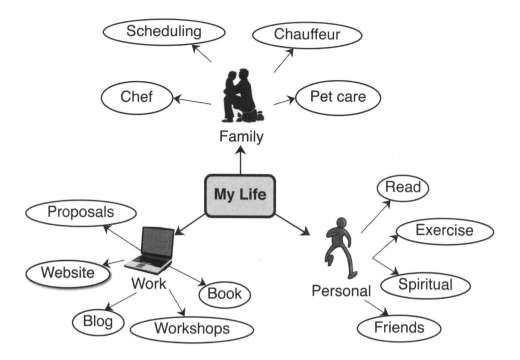

FIGURE 5.2. Web showing proper arrow direction.

level should share a similar conceptual weight. Nodes on the same level are known as **peers**. In our example, figure 5.2, "Family," "Work," and "Personal" are all peers that reside at Level 2 of the web and share the same parent, "My Life." This makes visual and conceptual sense because everything linked from the main topic of the web is a component of that main topic. In my professional experience, I have never worked with an individual who had any confusion "reading" a web that adhered to this rule.

No less fascinating is that when connections are reversed, a completely opposite effect occurs. While there is nothing technical to prevent a diagram from being drawn the opposite way—with arrows pointing in toward the main topic—it stops thinking in its tracks. Links that break Law #2 and go in the "wrong" direction make the web incoherent and can even make it indecipherable.

The visual power of the direction of links has to do with convergent and divergent thinking. To emphasize this point, contrast figure 5.2, with 5.3, shown below.

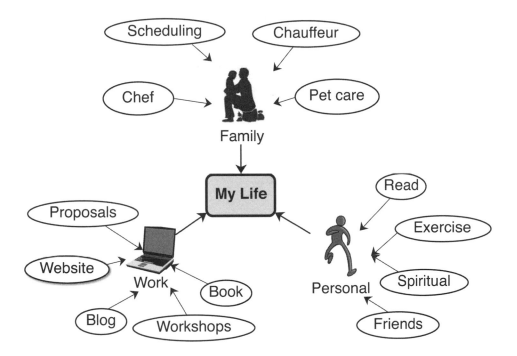

FIGURE 5.3. Convergent diagram of "My Life" with details.

Figure 5.2 is a proper web showing a main topic, three subtopics, and details. The Parent→Child relationship is clear. "My Life" has three main parts. Do you notice your eyes following the arrows outward from the center and scanning all of the branches of the web? This diagram models a divergent representation of the topic and encourages the viewer to explore further and consider what the next level of the web will be.

Figure 5.3, however, is profoundly different. Here the relationships are in fact Child→Parent. At first glance, both diagrams may seem to accurately depict the concept (just as the chocolate cake example in chapter 3 showed the ingredients), but look again. Do you find that you're visually encouraged to scan the whole web, or do you feel your eyes pulled toward the "My Life" node in the center? The direction of the arrows causes our eyes to converge on the answer. The key difference is that figure 5.3 models convergent thinking. The arrows lead to the main topic. There may be rare occasions to represent ideas in this way, but by and large, when arrows point inward, they literally and figuratively lead the learner to a dead end. The power of this law of visual literacy fully revealed itself to me when I was teaching webbing to my students. When I didn't instruct them not to, some would make arrows that pointed inward. On one occasion, I decided to do a spontaneous test and asked a first grader named Dahlia to come to the board, where I projected her "My Favorites" web on the screen.

When she was shown her diagram, figure 5.4, Dahlia promptly gave a perfectly nice oral summary to the class.

Using the web as a guide, Dahlia gleefully reported that her favorite

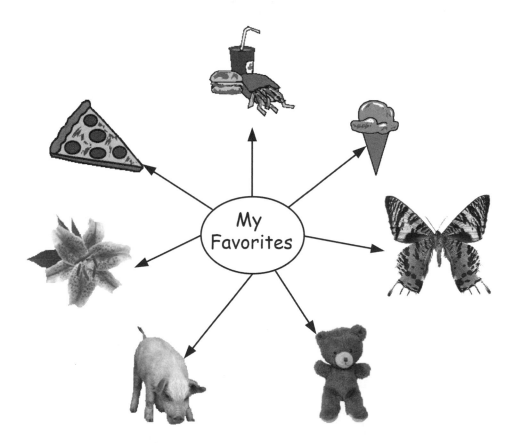

FIGURE 5.4. Web of "My Favorites," created by a first grader.

things included pizza, butterflies, teddy bears, and so on. She began to ad-lib on the various subtopics of the web to embellish her account.

After she finished her oral summary, I changed the direction of the arrows but left everything else the same (fig. 5.5). Then I asked her again to talk us through her diagram.

This time, the results were dramatically different. Dahlia was mute. She could not even begin to discuss what she saw. Her inability was especially profound because she had just finished doing the same oral presentation from the first web moments before. This time she was completely paralyzed.

In the first case (fig. 5.4), which modeled the concept with a divergent approach, the direction of the arrows guided her seamlessly from main

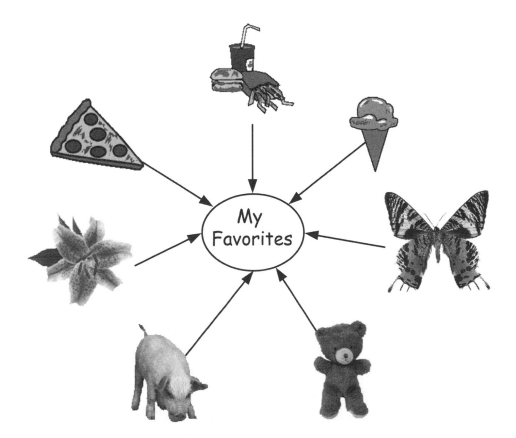

FIGURE 5.5. Convergent diagram of "My Favorites."

topic to each subtopic. This liberated her to speak fluidly and sequentially. The model showed her where to start and the arrows led her through the rest of the web.

In the second version (fig. 5.5), which models convergent thinking, the arrows, in effect, pointed Dahlia to where the story ended. It did not show her how to start. In this version, the story had seven possible beginnings, which stopped her in her tracks. For Dahlia, the links led to a dead end at the main idea. Her experience shows us the degree to which arrow direction drives the visual literacy of a diagram. It also reinforces our definition of a web. While many types of diagrams can be used to depict many types of information, a web must adhere to Law #2 because connections define the relationships between nodes, and the Parent→Child relationship creates the conceptual relationship:

Main topic → Subtopic

This relationship makes webbing an excellent go-to strategy for developing complex concepts and planning writing.

Connections in convergent diagrams model a Child→Parent relationship, which creates the conceptual relationship:

Subtopic → Main topic

This difference makes diagramming convergent thinking a less universal strategy, though it is still useful for visualizing ideas such as multiple causes for a single event. The act of convergent thinking plays a critical role in the process of organizing ideas visually because we invoke this type of thinking when we make decisions about how ideas fit together. Convergent and divergent thinking work together harmoniously to develop concepts that display a visual hierarchy of information; however, convergent thinking does not generally have to be mapped.

Dahlia taught us that there is a profound visual literacy to the direction of the connections in webs and mind maps, which clarifies the hierarchy of information being shown. Through our analysis, we acknowledged that while there are some valid reasons and occasions to graphically display convergent thinking, proper webs with outward pointing arrows offer much more versatility and provide a universal framework for developing ideas.

Law #3: Connections Never Close a Loop

The next essential law of webbing is that the **connections never close a loop**. Closing a loop is analogous to creating a circular argument. This graphic no-no will destroy the logic of a web and render its many virtues—productivity and clarity of message among them—useless. It's easy to prove why closing a loop is a fatal mistake in webbing. Figure 5.1, shown at the beginning of the chapter, is our standard, law-abiding web. It follows all the rules. In contrast, figure 5.6 is a *not* a semantic

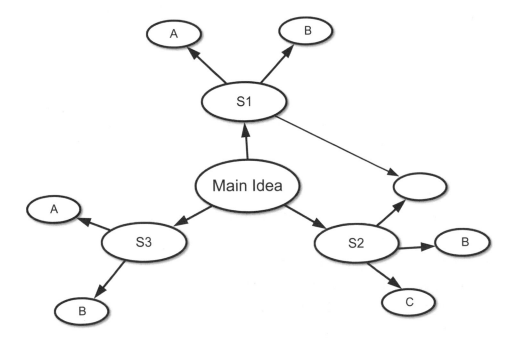

FIGURE 5.6. Closed web with a conceptual problem.

web. Perhaps more accurately, it could be called a semantic web with a big problem. Here, the subtopics and details are labeled and the problem spot is left blank.

This diagram has broken Law #3 by closing a loop. At a glance, this may not seem critically important and may even seem like a useful way to convey a relationship. This single link, however, ruins the logic of the web, and in doing so deteriorates its efficacy as a learning tool. One test of the importance of this law can be conducted informally. Ask yourself which web is easier to understand, figure 5.1 or 5.6? Which passes the eyeball test?

If you agree that figure 5.1 is clearer, let's ask ourselves why. Is it because figure 5.6 has an extra element (the arrow)? Perhaps it plays a role, but the essential reason is more interesting. By closing a loop, we create both a "right-brain" problem and a "left-brain" problem.

When a web has a closed loop, its logic is destroyed. In figure 5.6, subtopics S1 and S2 both link to the same detail. How can this detail link to two different subtopics (S1 and S2) at the same time? Should the blank node be "S1.C" or should it be "S2.A"? How does this dual connection affect the whole idea? It is not easy for our brains to reconcile, and it breaks sharply from the clarity of the web depicted in figure 5.1. The loop creates a left-brain conundrum. The logical left hemisphere seeks sequence and order, but the diagram creates a relationship that is illogical. For the left hemisphere, this amounts to conceptual chaos.

The second problem caused by breaking Law 3 relates to visual literacy. The right hemisphere focuses on the closed loop and stops seeing the topic as a whole. It takes effort to look away from the loop and study S3. Remember how Dahlia got stumped when arrows collapsed on the center node? The loop is also hard to look away from because we recognize it is a problem—it breaks from the visual Parent→Child order that is consistent throughout the rest of the web. This problem is magnified because it gives a disproportionate visual weight to the detail that we cannot logically label. As too much weight is given to this area of the map, the rest of the map gets too little. Our holistic, visual right hemisphere instantly identifies the loop as a problem with the overall concept, and will keep us looking there, while our analytical left hemisphere wrestles with the logic until we can untangle the problem and get the web straightened out. This is visual inquiry at work. Webs provide a way to look at ideas and puzzle with them that engages the logical left brain and the holistic right brain in the process of critical thinking.

Webs: Visual Outlines That Engage the Whole Mind

When the three laws of webbing are obeyed, webs and mind maps correlate to traditional outlines. This is a potent symbiotic relationship that naturally marries big-picture right-brain thinking with sequential left-brain thinking. The incredible fact that webs and mind maps are "visual outlines" can transform academic performance.

> When the three laws of webbing are obeyed, webs and mind maps correlate to traditional outlines. This is a potent symbiotic relationship that naturally marries big-picture right-brain thinking with sequential left-brain thinking.

The importance of this relationship cannot be understated. By teaching students to think visually, we also arm them with a blueprint for completing sequential tasks like writing. Most students despise outlining. They hate it for a lot of reasons, but one important reason is that it does not match the way they think, so it is often hard or even impossible to do. Outlining, by definition, requires that an idea follow a sequence, so to do it effectively, the learner needs to know the precise order of every component of that idea. We already proved that thinking does not follow a linear path. However, a sequence of ideas like an outline is precisely what is needed in order to write and complete linear tasks.

When we teach our students to combine visual thinking—as a strategy to get ideas out of their heads—with its more buttoned-down and orderly fraternal twin, the outline, we will have fulfilled our mission as teachers because our students will have mastered a skill that lets them use their whole mind to think critically and act productively.

Below is an image of a web together with its corresponding outline (fig. 5.7). The web is highly effective as a bridge to a traditional linear outline and as a way to harness divergent and covergent thinking.

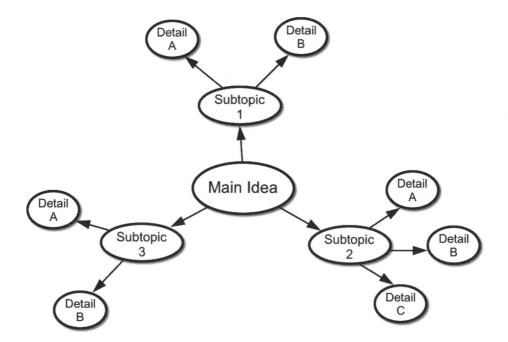

FIGURE 5.7. Web–outline relationship.

Main Idea
I.   Subtopic 1
     A. Detail A
     B. Detail B
II. Subtopic 2
     A. Detail A
     B. Detail B
     C. Detail C
III. Subtopic 3
     A. Detail A
     B. Detail B

Using the web–outline relationship improves productivity and achievement because it allows learners to think as they naturally do, using visual processes to conceive and structure ideas, and using outlining to further refine the best order for subtopics in a paper—or whatever final form that idea needs to take. This process is magical because it allows learners to use exactly the type of thinking required for whatever part of the task they need to complete. Creative, divergent brainstorming gets the puzzle pieces on the table, and convergent sequential thinking finds the way they fit together.

Webs and outlines are like two sides of a coin. They are also like the two hemispheres of the brain. The diagram side is the visual right brain. It is "heads." The linear left brain is the outline. It is "tails." They are complementary and inextricably related. By teaching learners to flip the coin and toggle between lateral, divergent thinking and vertical, convergent thinking, we can empower them to take advantage of their full range of cognitive assets and unlock the puzzle of learning.

CHAPTER 6

Evaluating Ideas with Visual Inquiry

Semantic webs and mind maps provide visual clues that help learners evaluate the strengths and weaknesses of the content their webs represent. By studying the appearance of the diagram, students and teachers can glean insights and see how to address areas of need. This method of evaluation is an act of visual inquiry, and a few design guidelines can have a powerful impact on how creating diagrams facilitates this type of metacognition. These guidelines are:

1. Use one word (or phrase) per bubble.
2. Create meaning with color and image.
3. Compose ideas with visual balance.

Use One Word (or Phrase) Per Bubble

Distilling an idea into a bare-bones web—which eliminates most core words and leaves the meaningful fringe words—is challenging. A person who can execute the task, however, will have gained complete command of the content he is mapping. Newcomers to visual thinking have a tendency to put too many words into their webs. Some are even inclined to write sentences. This is a mistake. There is a time and place for sentences, but it's not when making the diagram. Here are a number of benefits to limiting any node to one word or, at most, one phrase.

1. Too many words make a web cluttered. They detract from the simplicity the web conveys. People are comfortable reading and comfortable looking, but when diagrams force us to do both, they communicate information less effectively and detract from the visual structure of the concept.

2. Distilling ideas into single words forces the creator to focus on essential content that adds meaning to the overall idea. The act of constructing the web compels the creator to make numerous decisions about the organization and hierarchy of information in a topic. By forcing the author to distill nodes to one word or phrase, webbing ensures that the learner focuses on essential elements and removes extraneous information.

3. A sentence in a node of a web can contain more than one idea, thus masking crossed logic or intertwined ideas. When two ideas are embedded in a single node, the web's power to keep the concept clear is lost. Using single words instead of sentences prevents this problem.

4. Single words allow the creator to easily move or reorder the idea, and they serve as placeholders for full sentences that can be written later. Words that represent sentences can be moved more easily than full sentences.

5. Webs are supposed to be a fast and fluid way to work that matches how we think. Using one word per node keeps the mind focused on developing the idea and prevents the author from becoming sidetracked by the process of writing.

6. Webs have their own visual grammar and do not need sentences to convey meaning.

Two examples illustrate these points. In both depictions, the creator broke down the content, but one is more effective than the other. The first example is the visual representation of a paragraph about a Hawaiian island[1] (fig. 6.1).

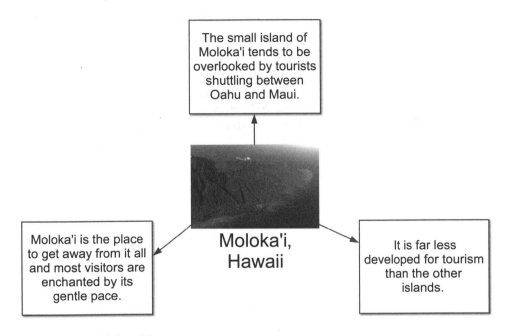

The small island of Moloka'i tends to be overlooked by tourists shuttling between Oahu and Maui.

Moloka'i, Hawaii

Moloka'i is the place to get away from it all and most visitors are enchanted by its gentle pace.

It is far less developed for tourism than the other islands.

FIGURE 6.1. Web with sentences.

This web contains forty-six words. It contains unnecessary words and whole sentences, and each node has more than one piece of information. The viewer has to study each node separately and read the three statements. The creator of this web may have copied and pasted text into the nodes, negating the benefit a learner reaps through the process of editing away text and distilling the idea into essential words. This web also detracts from the content because it is neither a clear paragraph nor a simple diagram. Essentially, the whole is less than the sum of its parts.

The second web contains ten words (fig. 6.2). It includes all of the key information found in the original text, but this time the creator distilled the ideas into single words within each node. While the viewer still needs to read the words to learn the content, engaging with this

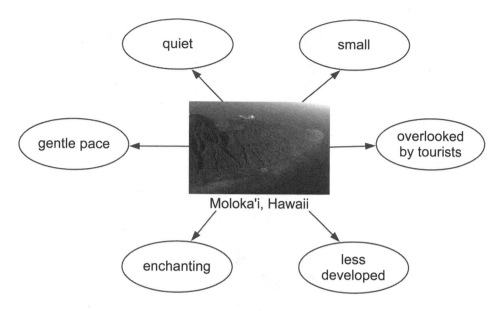

FIGURE 6.2. Web with essential words.

web does not feel like a normal act of reading. In contrast, it is a holistic visual act in which the eyes take in the entire idea at one glance. This diagram allows the content to be conveyed clearly in a representation not dominated by text.

Concise and clear communication is at the heart of the value of visual thinking. The only grammar in webs is visual, and the only words in webs are essential. A web can be considered a skeletal representation of an idea. It serves as the bones that hold the idea together until it can be fleshed out into a final deliverable, whether that is a paragraph, essay, oral presentation, or something different.

> The only grammar in webs is visual, and the only words in webs are essential.

I have told at least a thousand teachers and students, "Trust the web. It won't lie." More accurately, a web cannot get away with a lie because the process eliminates 80 to 99 percent of the words needed to represent an idea in sentence form. With so few words, the words that remain are meaningful. In a web with one idea per bubble, there can be no ambiguity of thought because only essential elements and key ideas are shown. Any weakness or imprecision is exposed.

Written work can mask a lack of conceptual understanding or suffer by being disorganized. When an idea is well constructed visually before the writing is done, it will be well organized conceptually. When such an idea is fleshed out into a paper (or an essay or a project), it will be strong work.

Create Meaning with Color and Image

In webs and maps, color, symbols, and images are more than decorative elements. They create a visual language that adds meaning and facilitates visual inquiry. Our look at memory and dual code theory explained why a picture together with text is easier to remember than text alone.

The mind map that follows is the composite work of a group of ninth graders I taught (fig. 6.3). It is from a general science class and depicts six types of simple machines. Students added symbols to represent the machines, in some cases including a third-level node that exemplified how the machines are used. Creating the mind map was an engaging way for them to show what they had learned. It gave them a solid understanding of the scope of the topic and multiple ways to remember the material.

In creating this map, students used more than visual and spatial intelligence—web making is a kinesthetic and affective experience too. Even when done with a computer, the experience is tactile. Authors move pieces around like a puzzle to create an idea that fits together. It is also an affective experience because the students used images, shapes, and colors in a personally meaningful layout to represent their ideas.

In the "Simple Machines" mind map example, the students made

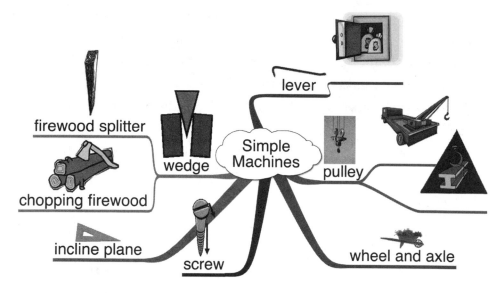

FIGURE 6.3. "Simple Machines" mind map.

choices and decisions about how to represent the idea. Visual thinking initiated a process steeped in personal expression and authentic connection to the idea. Does this process make it easier to learn,
understand, and remember? Of course it does. Do the choices show a
high degree of understanding? Absolutely. The students' depiction of
simple machines demonstrates something approaching a generative
knowledge of the content. The mind map could serve as an assessment indicating that they could apply their understanding. The next
application of this content should probably involve using the real
things! The creative process inherent in this approach to learning
engages virtually all of the senses and makes learning relevant. By
choosing colors and images, and making all of the decisions that go
into visual representations, students forge a personal connection to
the content that requires analysis and fosters understanding. The outcome of the process—whether a web or a map—is a creative expression, the highest level of critical thinking according to Bloom's Revised
Taxonomy (fig. 6.4).

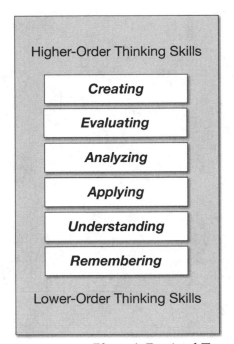

FIGURE 6.4. Bloom's Revised Taxonomy

Compose Ideas with Visual Balance

Strong diagrams possess a visual balance and a compositional unity. The layout enhances visual literacy and makes visual inquiry easier. For instance, the composition of the diagram can indicate areas of emphasis and the sequence of ideas. Of immense value to the learner, however, is that the composition can also reveal gaps in understanding or lapses in organization. It can even let the learner "see" a gap in an idea. This unique property of webbing makes it exceptional for metacognition.

We can gain a better understanding of how to create webs that transform learning with a short art lesson, courtesy of Leonardo da Vinci. Artists use various conventions to move a viewer's eyes around a painting, and we can use the same techniques with mind maps and webs. In the *Mona Lisa*, da Vinci used a technique called "pyramidal

FIGURE 6.5. *Mona Lisa* showing pyramidal composition.

composition" to build the painting (fig. 6.5). Mona Lisa is centrally placed on the canvas with her head toward the top, elbows spread wide, and hands crossed at the bottom. The crossed hands and the twist of the head create a visual flow that steers the eyes through the composition so the viewer absorbs the entire picture and is then visually pulled around the masterpiece again, absorbing more details each time.[2] The spacing and positioning of the elements create a visual rhythm that engages the viewer in the whole picture, and many of these principles can be applied to diagramming an idea.

Luckily, we don't have to be da Vinci to make effective mind maps and semantic webs. We can simply take the principles of balance, movement, and space together with some consideration of color, shape, and

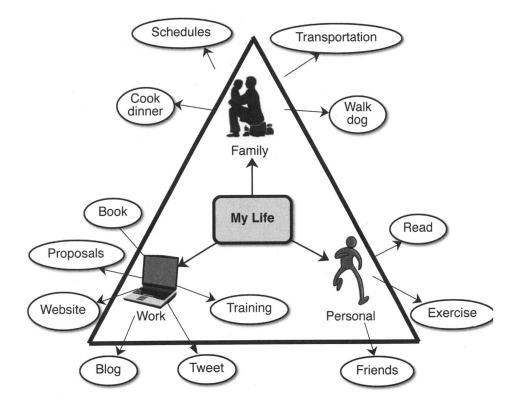

FIGURE 6.6. "My Life" web with pyramidal construction.

image to create webs that help us learn and also convey meaning to others.

Above is another rendition of the "My Life" web (fig. 6.6). In this version the subtopics are defined, and even though they do not all have precisely the same amount of detail, there is a visual balance. It is important to emphasize this point with students, so they do not become overly focused on having equal numbers of details or a specific number of subtopics.

The diagram is a picture of a typical week in my life. I strive for a healthy life–work balance, and a glance at the web tells me how I'm doing. Visual unity and balance are conveyed through evenly spaced subtopics, similar numbers of details, and a cohesive visual language.

The conventions I chose to create a unified symbolic language include ovals for details, a round-edged rectangle for the main idea, and images for the subtopics. These features allow the eye to move easily from topic to topic and take in the whole picture. The use of relevant images that are in a consistent style and scale creates harmony in the overall aesthetic. The result is a web that is comfortable to look at and conveys a lot of information, yet is simple to decipher and understand.

Another guideline for visualizing a cohesive idea is to think about the spacing of hierarchical levels as orbitals around the main topic. As nodes lie farther out from the middle, they represent more granular details of the topic. Orbitals are a visual cue that helps to ensure that nodes on each orbital have the same conceptual weight. Adhering to this visual principle makes it easy to develop a topic with parallel construction and to notice when organization breaks down.

> Orbitals are a visual cue that helps to ensure that nodes on each orbital have the same conceptual weight—this visual principle makes it easy to develop a topic with parallel construction and to notice when organization breaks down.

In figure 6.7, "Family," "Work," and "Personal" are all Level 2 subtopics of the "My Life" web. They exist at the same hierarchical level and have the same conceptual weight within the overall topic. The web looks unified because the symbolic language is consistent and also because all of the Level 2 nodes are more or less on the same orbital. The same holds true for "Walk dog," "Exercise," and "Book." These details are all Level 3 nodes, and visually they also reside on the same orbital. The orbital is a practical aesthetic guideline that adds visual literacy and aids visual inquiry, but orbitals do not *create* the hierarchy of an idea. The logic of the web that corresponds to a traditional outline is created only by the links.

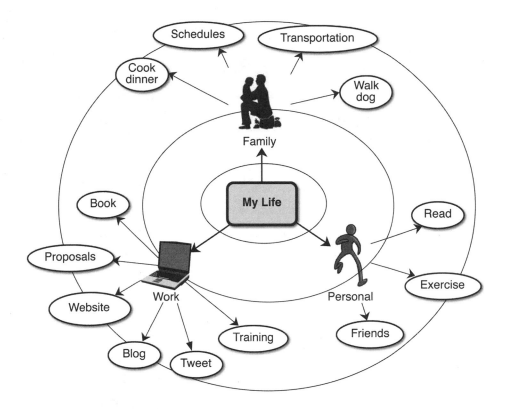

FIGURE 6.7. "My Life" web with orbitals that compose the hierarchy of information.

This example (fig 6.7) models an effective web that conveys a balanced idea. It is easy to evaluate the content and infer the meaning because the web shows one idea per node, uses image and shape to clarify content, and is visually balanced. The act of creating the web also provides instantaneous formative feedback. Maps and webs allow the creator to look at the idea in progress, reflect upon it in real time, and address any lapses in organizational logic or information gaps that the map reveals.

Mind (Map) the "Gap"

By looking at your web you can see where you stand with your idea, for better or for worse. This makes webbing an intuitive way to evaluate an idea and a powerful metacognitive strategy. With a glance, you can immediately see which areas are developed or underdeveloped, and where gaps in logic or evidence may exist. Visual inquiry allows you to use your own optical analysis to examine your ideas and ask yourself whether it represents the idea you are trying to convey.

To see this principle in practice, we will examine a "My Life" example from a different week (fig. 6.8).

It is pretty obvious why this was a rough week. There were several extra family and work requirements, and no time for the personal things that give life balance. This web, in its own dispassionate way, provides a way to analyze the information and determine what is missing. The

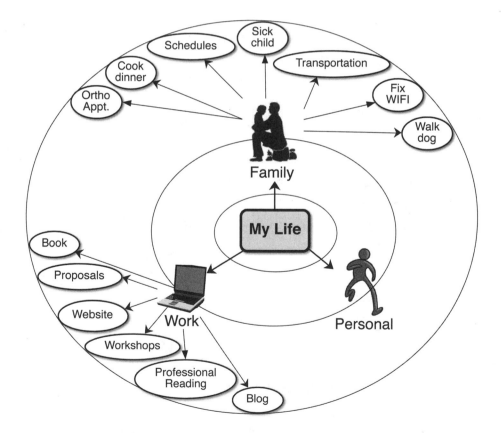

FIGURE 6.8. Orbitals help show the gap in the web.

"visible gap" illustrates where the problem lies by revealing empty space. By extension, the gap is prescriptive. It provides insight into what needs to change to solve the problem and reveals enough clues to devise a plan to address it.

Webbing strategies are wonderful for personal analysis, and the same principle applies to scholastic content. As teachers and students focus on the information they can glean from visual gaps, they can become independent problem solvers and advanced practitioners capable of sophisticated evaluation. We can teach students to look for gaps to help them reflect on the status of their learning.

The web below is based on reading notes from an article about the box turtle (fig. 6.9). It indicates that the learner had a sufficient amount of knowledge about threats, food, and life cycle, but the web was not balanced. This imbalance makes it clear that "habitat" needs additional information.

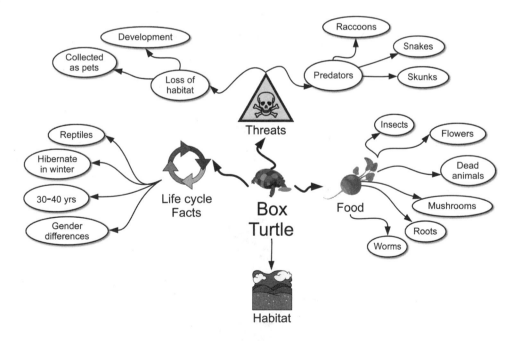

FIGURE 6.9. Box turtle web.

In the second iteration, the student was able to address this gap through additional targeted research because it was known exactly what information was missing (fig. 6.10).

The ability to see a gap—identify what is missing—is a remarkable cognitive leap and one of the highest forms of critical thinking that exists. It represents a huge advantage for individuals who are able to do it. This is what innovators and problem solvers do; they identify something lacking and they fill the void. Some get rich in the process; others quietly improve things with no fanfare or monetary reward. By teaching students how to distill ideas and to reflect on what is shown and what is missing, we can give them the tools to be great innovators and critical thinkers.

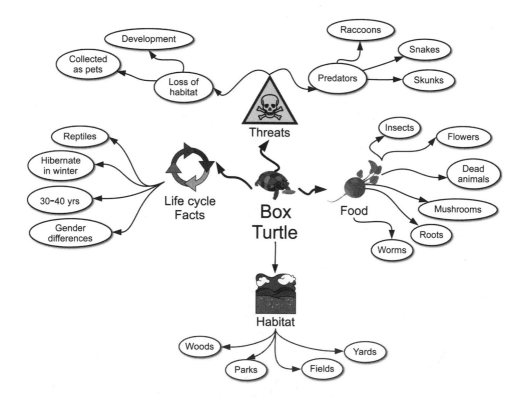

FIGURE 6.10. Fully developed box turtle web.

Parallel Construction and Hierarchical Balance

One of the most complicated aspects of organizing complex ideas is the prioritization of information. Webbing and mind-mapping strategies let people use their eyes for this purpose and engage them to do what they do best—looking for patterns, making predictions, seeing connections, and identifying relationships. It is easy to compose ideas with parallel structure using webs because links that define the levels of the idea are easy to see. It is possible, however, to deviate from this principle and fail to notice when organization goes awry. In these cases, it is not uncommon for two nodes with different conceptual weights to end up on the same hierarchical level, leading to poor organization. The web below highlights this problem and provides some guidelines on how to fix it (fig. 6.11). Looking at the "My Life" example, the new subtopic,

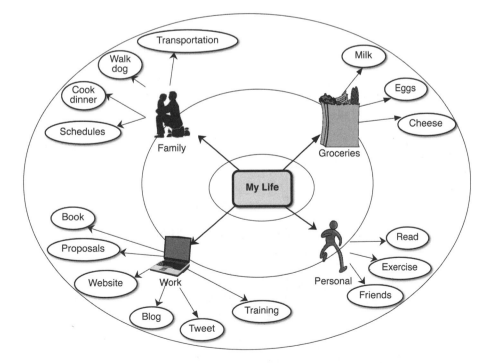

FIGURE 6.11. Web with a conceptual imbalance.

"Groceries," is not the conceptual equal of "Family" or "Work" or "Personal." It should probably be a detail of the category called "Family."

This example (fig 6.11) highlights a subtle point about visual thinking. Even when a web has visual balance and follows the laws of webbing, it can still have organizational problems.

Fortunately, because webs represent ideas in such a distilled fashion, this type of lapse is generally fairly easy to identify and correct. The creator can just drag "Groceries" over to where it belongs and change the symbols as needed. The ability to evaluate the structure of an idea visually is a powerful attribute of the webbing process.

In the example below, a different issue can be seen. The circled area shows where a student had trouble making decisions about subtopics (fig. 6.12). A burst of divergent thinking can result in a lot of information to organize; however, the convergent process of fitting it together can be difficult. Because webbing allows the entire topic to be seen at once, the student can more easily analyze it and determine that the construction is not parallel. The conceptual weight and level of detail of

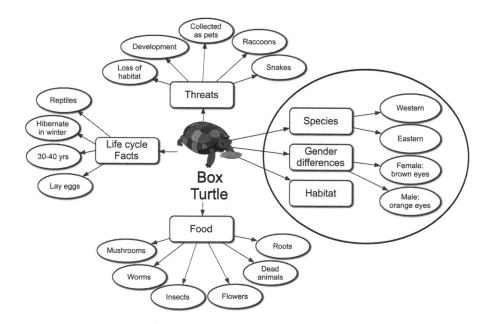

FIGURE 6.12. Web with a problem with parallel construction.

the circled area do not match that of the other subtopics. Visual inquiry revealed this problem, enabling the learner to make the necessary revisions to present a cohesive idea. The process required reevaluating the subtopics, making decisions about content, and deleting information that, while not wrong, was extraneous.

The web provided visual cues that identified where the concept was out of alignment and gave the creator a framework to address the problems. As an added benefit, this realization occurred while the creator was developing the idea, not when she was deeply involved in the writing process. As a strategy to get an idea out of one's head and into a workable format, webbing has no equal.

Closing Thoughts on Webbing

The remarkable ability of visual thinking to foster metacognition and self-evaluation makes me wonder why it isn't common practice in upper grades, in college, in careers, and at all levels of education. Sadly, the deliberate use of visual thinking declines as students reach higher grade levels. This is a costly mistake because webbing is so versatile and makes learning so much easier. Since it engages the whole mind in critical thinking, its use should be increased as concepts and academic tasks get more complex.

Instead of increasing in use as concepts and academic tasks get more complex, the use of visual thinking approaches declines as students reach higher grade levels. This is a costly mistake.

I can't be certain why visual inquiry is used less often at the upper grade levels, but I have a few ideas based on experience and observation. One possibility is that teachers and instructors of these age groups do not consider visual thinking to be a serious approach to academic study. It is accepted as valuable for teaching younger children and students with special needs, but there seems to be a time between middle school and high school when this changes. The perception seems to be that, because learning visually is creative, like drawing, it can't possibly be appropriate for performing sophisticated academic tasks.

One former student of mine told me that his high school teacher specifically didn't want him to use webbing because it was supposedly only for younger kids, and that a high school kid shouldn't need such a crutch! Clearly, this teacher is misguided. The goal of education can no longer be to create production-oriented automatons that mechanically execute learning tasks faster than the competition. In one of the many astute points Daniel Pink makes in his essential book *A Whole New Mind*, he explains that computers will always compute faster and global competition will work more cheaply. The goal of education today, therefore, is to give students the tools to learn their own way so that they can solve novel problems, ask complex questions, and design better solutions. These are the types of challenges that visual strategies prepare students to tackle because they refocus education on how to learn, not what to learn.

Many teachers may find this transition messy and unpredictable at first. Taking the Visual Leap represents a significant change in educational ethos and practice. Visual strategies feel different because they engage different parts of the brain than what much of school has traditionally called upon. But do not fear. Teaching your students to think the way they are naturally designed to is like giving a baby a bottle. It requires little explanation. They will quickly know what to do.

The final section of the book puts the theory into practice and provides an explicit process for teaching visual thinking that I hope will be simple and easy to integrate into your teaching practice.

PART 3

Teaching Visual Thinking

Teaching students to think visually is exhilarating and empowering because they "get it" so quickly. The process itself provides an instant "aha" moment for many learners, who, for the first time, see how their ideas can fit together. Appreciation for their newfound skill will grow rapidly as they realize that it simplifies virtually any learning experience.

Rebecca, a former student, in typical middle-school fashion, resisted when I first suggested that she web her idea before writing. Predictably, she complained that it was an extra step. Later (in a moment I have savored for more than a decade) she told me, "I hate to admit it, but that made that paper so much easier." A senior at an urban Philadelphia high school came up to me after a lesson and told me he "needed to learn how to do that." A New York City teacher told me she could use this method for teaching "just about anything." Naturally, I'm pleased that people see these methods as practical and transformative.

There is a dirty little secret, however, that I need to share: visual inquiry methods don't just make learning easier for students; they also make teaching easier. These methods can slash your preparation time because webbing is faster than making slideshow-type files. More importantly, visual thinking fosters rich learning experiences—particularly in the areas of student speaking, listening, and critical thinking—because it puts the messy role of organizing and processing concepts in the hands of the students, where it needs to be! This allows you, the teacher, to do more listening and guiding in class, which takes a lot less energy than teacher talk.

This final section of the book explains how you can teach your students to think visually and how you can use these strategies in class. The emphasis will be on using the skill of visual inquiry to improve writing, listening, note taking, and reading comprehension.

Chapters 7 and 8 explain how to teach visual thinking using the BOWL and LADLE process. This set of explicit steps for visualizing ideas provides a foundation for using visual inquiry in almost any context, whether that context is listening, planning, reading, or writing.

Chapter 9 models four grand-slam visual thinking classroom strategies: the Webstorm, the Reverse Mind Map, Summary Man, and Puzzle Prompt. Chapter 10 applies the principles of visual inquiry as a note-taking strategy that improves active listening and comprehension. Chapter 11 provides numerous classroom activities, examples, and templates to inspire and facilitate your Visual Leap.

CHAPTER 7

Introducing BOWL and LADLE: Perfect Utensils for Visual Thinking

Visual thinking begins with the assumption that concepts and topics can be represented visually and that this approach to organizing them helps learning. Radial diagrams like webs and mind maps are especially useful because they correspond to traditional outlines. This trait makes them the perfect bridge between nonlinear tasks (like brainstorming and formulating ideas) and linear tasks (like writing) because they allow learners to use both divergent and convergent thinking to process information. The next big question we will answer is how to do it.

The Webstorm

The **Webstorm** is the visual thinking method used by Marguerite and shown in the proof of nonlinear thinking, both in chapter 4. It is the core process of developing an idea from scratch and representing it as a completed web. The Webstorm is Visual Thinking 101. It uses a step-by-step process that can be easily taught and learned. For links to videos of the Webstorm process and for additional support, see the resources section of the book.

> The Webstorm gives teachers a valuable way to explore an idea with a group, and it gives individuals a powerful way to get started on a project and achieve a goal.

The Webstorm gets its name from the combination of the words "web" and "brainstorm." Like brainstorms, Webstorms begin with a creative burst of nonlinear thinking that draws out lots of information. Unlike brainstorms, the Webstorm process leverages assets of both sides of the mind to guide ideas into an organized format, giving teachers a valuable way to explore an idea with a group and giving individuals a powerful way to get started on a project and achieve a goal.

Brainstorm Versus Webstorm

Brainstorm	Webstorm
• Generally uses pen and paper to capture and communicate ideas to group	• Generally uses technology to capture and communicate ideas to group
• Engages participants to add content	• Engages participants to add content
• Activates prior knowledge of the topic	• Activates prior knowledge of the topic
• Promotes rich debate and dialogue about the topic	• Promotes rich debate and dialogue that can be captured and logically integrated into the diagram
	• Uses images and links to produce a visually structured and cohesive idea
	• Can be converted into an outline and easily used to write

The BOWL and LADLE Process

The best way to Webstorm is to use a process I call the **BOWL and LADLE**. The BOWL and LADLE procedure is as good for critical thinking as Grandma's chicken soup is for a cold. Because it uses visual inquiry, the BOWL and LADLE accomplishes heavy cognitive lifting that doesn't feel hard. It's comfort food for the active mind. The BOWL and LADLE makes it easy to cook up well-developed ideas that are easy to digest.

In a classroom, the ideal way to use the BOWL and LADLE process is to project a computer or tablet screen so that students can see it easily and to use a software program that allows words and pictures to be added to the screen and easily moved around. Depending on the size of the group involved, 8½" x 11" paper, pens, and tape can also work. Individuals could even use sticky notes to construct their webs. Interactive whiteboard software can work well. Mind mapping and visual thinking software and some tablet apps and web tools are ideal for this purpose. My recommendations for tools that facilitate visual thinking are detailed in the resources section at the end of the book.

The BOWL and LADLE process has three phases (fig. 7.1). In this chapter, we'll explore the first phase in detail, looking at how to develop ideas into webs. The second and third phases, examined in chapter 8, explain how to refine the idea and detail three of the deliverables that webs can help students create.

The BOWL and LADLE will serve you well for academic learning, professional responsibilities, and personal planning. The process is a straightforward way to develop skills in visual thinking. It also builds analytical and problem-solving skills because once you master it, you will likely go beyond the procedure outlined here and use visual approaches to attack new and unforeseen questions in novel ways. When you believe that problems can be analyzed visually and you trust your skill in visual inquiry to guide you, you will have accessed a new level of intellectual potential and will have taken the Visual Leap.

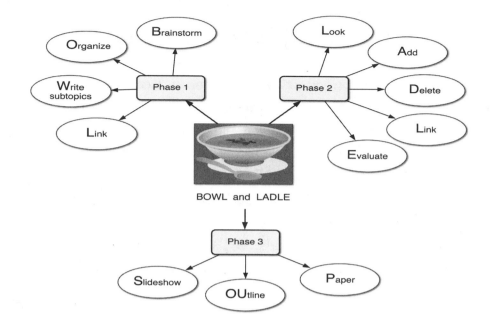

FIGURE 7.1. BOWL and LADLE process.

Shaping the BOWL

I'll model the process for forming the BOWL using the topic of "My Diet." To get the most out of the experience, complete the steps yourself as we move through the process. In addition, consider the content you teach, an example that would work well for you, and what tools you might use. Download an app from the list in the resources section, or use one of the software or web tools I recommend.

If you find it too cumbersome to read a book, learn to use a software tool, and acquire a teaching strategy all at once, just use a piece of paper. After you have a sense of the process, take your time to execute it with software, as you would in class. Once you become experienced with this approach to visual thinking, you may find, as I have, that it is the best way to start any project, from writing a lesson to planning a new instructional unit to mapping curriculum. Whatever the context, the BOWL and LADLE process efficiently promotes clear thinking.

Procedure

1. Open your visual thinking software or get your pencil and paper ready. If you are using paper and pencil, turn the paper sideways (landscape).
2. Add a central node and name it "My Diet." This will be the main idea, your Level 1 concept in your web (fig 7.2).
3. Follow the BOWL procedure detailed in the remainder of this chapter; continue with the step-by-step LADLE procedure explained in chapter 8.

PHASE 1: BOWL

Brainstorm Organize Write Subtopics Link

Step 1: Brainstorm

In the **Brainstorm**, you will ask students for everything they can think of about the topic and put it on the map. This is a high-energy, divergent-thinking activity during which you should add information freely, without any concern about whether it is right or wrong or relevant. The goal of the brainstorming phase is to allow students to add anything they can about the topic and to dump it onto the screen.

When teaching, you will prompt the students with the essential question and ask them about the topic—in this case, "My Diet," which includes the foods and drinks they consumed in the last few days. Add the responses to the map. Often, it takes about two to five minutes before students become saturated and cannot add more.

Go ahead and try this for yourself now. Give yourself two minutes to write down everything, randomly spaced on the screen.

Make sure to add items as **unlinked nodes**. These may be called **"floating nodes"** or **"floating topics"** in different software tools. Many visual thinking tools add links and connect nodes automatically. *It is very important to use a tool that allows floating nodes.* If this feature cannot be disabled, then it may not be the best tool for visual inquiry. All of the tools I recommend can create "floating nodes."

The floating nodes in the Brainstorm phase are critical because you can work with them as discrete pieces of information at the same conceptual level. This is absolutely essential to the Webstorm process (and for most of the activities promoted in this book). In the Brainstorm phase, all of the nodes are equal.

The reason this is so important goes back to the science of learning and the proof of nonlinear thinking. Each node begins as an ingredient of a concept, and not part of a cohesive idea. When we are in the brainstorming phase, we are gathering information, not making decisions

FIGURE 7.2. Webstorm Step 1: Brainstorm.

about how it will fit in our final representation of the idea. This important detail ensures that we thoroughly separate the cognitive task of
"remembering" from the task of "evaluating." This distinction will be
important as we develop our idea.

For the time being, all nodes added should be unlinked. Thus, all
nodes enter the idea at the same hierarchical level. The level of the
nodes will change as we work with the topic, but the diagram needs to
start out this way.

If you are working with sticky notes or paper and tape, *add only one
word per piece of paper.* This will be important when we begin to group
and sort information.

Below is my brainstorm of "My Diet" after two minutes (fig. 7.3).
How does it compare with yours?

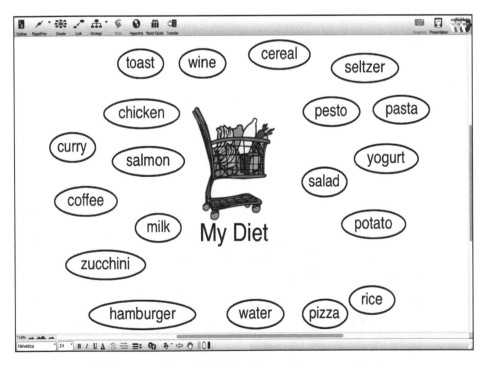

FIGURE 7.3. Webstorm Step 1: Brainstorm after two minutes.

Interpretation and Analysis

After two minutes, I was struggling to think of more things to add. Were you?

My first recall phase was a vigorous burst, but it was soon over. When this happens to you (now) or your students (when you lead this in class)—and it will—listen to your brain and acknowledge this lull in energy. The slowdown comes when you reach maximum cognitive load and have no more mental capacity to think about that question or to keep the idea bouncing around in working memory. We get to this point because our minds are not computers and cannot steadily, rapidly continue to compute. Mental saturation happens to individuals working alone and to groups working collaboratively. The human mind continually needs new triggers and new stimulation to nourish the thinking process and refresh cognitive load.

The brainstorm process may last longer than two minutes in a group activity because students will feed off one another as new ideas prompt recall. When you brainstorm as an individual, you will probably run out of ideas sooner. As a guideline, it is a good time to make an adjustment when things slow down.

If you reach this first slowdown when there is a critical mass of nodes on the screen—enough to manipulate and work with—it is time to move to Step 2. If there is a dearth of content, and the ideas would barely be enough to generate more discussion or analysis, then ask a few leading questions. In this example, you could try, "What did you eat this morning? Last night? Name something in your cupboard. What's in your fridge?" Naturally, most academic Webstorm activities will not cover such familiar content, but *prompting questions* and *teacher wait time* are two strategies you should call on to get the most out of this step of the exercise. (An exception, however, is when teaching the Webstorm to students as a learning strategy. In this case, I strongly recommend using familiar content so students can quickly grasp the process of visual thinking.)

Step 2: Organize

After completing the Brainstorm and generating enough ideas to work with, we will begin to **Organize** them by grouping and sorting. Grouping consists of dragging items that belong together into piles on the screen. Critical thinking enters in the organization phase, because we will make decisions about our idea based on the details we see. As we drag our symbols around, our idea will start to come together. This process will lead to a cohesive and well-organized visualization of our topic. The previous chart of Bloom's Revised Taxonomy (fig 6.4) makes this transition clear. *Remembering* and *understanding* characterized the Brainstorm. In the Organize step, Webstormers begin to *analyze* and *evaluate* the information by making decisions about it.

I recommend several prompts to get students involved in this process. They are all variations of the same idea, which is to challenge students to look for patterns in the content and group the information on the screen. Here are a few I use frequently:

- What do you see that you can group together?
- Which items relate?
- Do you see groups of things that look like they should go together?
- Can you identify things that might be in the same category?
- Can you move bubbles into piles that make sense together?

These questions challenge students to seek patterns and test hypotheses about the information they see. They also prompt students to think independently and trust their intuition, which builds academic confidence. The visual analysis and pattern recognition that occur in the Organize phase represent critical thinking; however, it is so fluid and intuitive that it may not feel like it to the students or even the teacher. The organization step usually begins quickly and easily, but because information can be grouped in different ways, decisions must be made about how the idea will evolve. These decisions are the seeds of critical thinking that will sprout into debate and rich student dialogue as students probe deeper into their analysis and provide explanations for their reasoning. For this reason, while the BOWL and LADLE process is inherently visual, it also directly enhances speaking and listening skills. The high-quality student dialogue that the Webstorm produces makes teaching significantly easier.

> Visual analysis and pattern recognition represent critical thinking; however, it is so fluid and intuitive that it may not feel like it.

To organize the web, ask students to direct you to drag together floating nodes that belong in the same group. If you are Webstorming as an individual, you will probably have a fairly clear idea of how to start organizing your idea. If, on the other hand, you are Webstorming with a class, many surprises can emerge because individuals will see different patterns in the information and different ways to approach the material. If you are using paper and pens to do this activity, spread out the sheets on the floor or a wall as needed to create the groups you see. Write only one idea per piece of paper, so that the items can be moved around freely.

After grouping my web, this is what it looked like (fig. 7.4). How does it compare with yours?

Interpretation and Analysis

The Organize step is a lively moment in class discussions. You may be surprised by how quickly and intensely debate begins during this phase, as students immediately encounter decision-making challenges because of the blurry lines and complexity inherent in most ideas. As

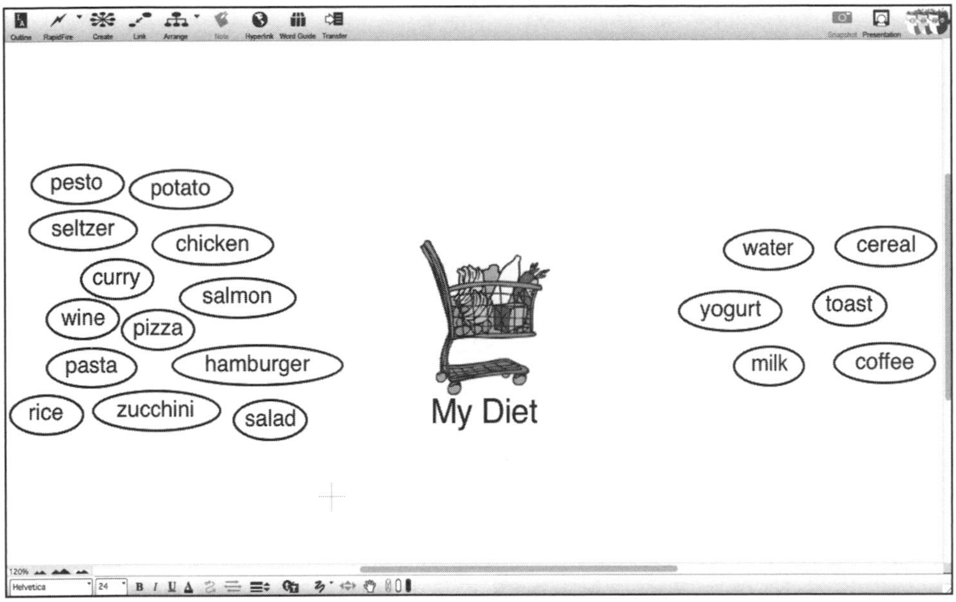

FIGURE 7.4. Webstorm Step 2: Organize.

a teacher, you will find that you can use the Webstorm process with a broad range of content as you transition to the Common Core State Standards because it offers a clear way to integrate into daily instruction decision making, supporting assertions with evidence, and debating with respect and good citizenship.

Figure 7.4 was my first stab at grouping my ideas. I put nodes into two piles, which I grouped as breakfast and dinner. Someone else might organize them differently, for example, the four food groups (fig. 7.5). Here it gets pretty interesting: Which is right? Which offers more compelling evidence? Which answers the question more effectively? The answer is obvious: neither is inherently more accurate or effective. The decisions that led to each of these visualizations are perfectly reasonable, and both types of organization can be supported by evidence.

Evidence-based decision making is a powerful skill that lies at the heart of complex thought and is a skill that the Webstorm teaches naturally. These two versions demonstrate how differently two individuals

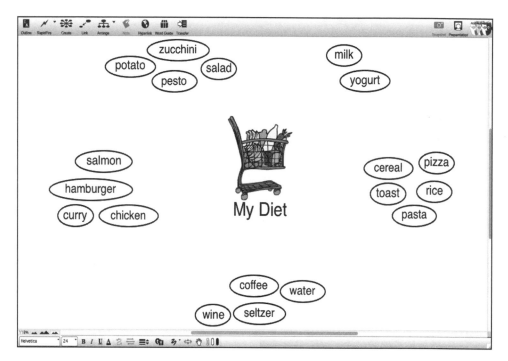

FIGURE 7.5. Alternative organization of a Webstorm.

might interpret facts and see patterns in ideas. Alternative conclusions can evolve from the same facts, a point that is a critical component of debate, persuasion, and reasoned argument. In a classroom setting, or even while working alone, this dichotomy will create an authentic opportunity for meaningful debate and deep thinking, as individuals seek to persuade others (and/or themselves) that their organization is best.

The fact that people organize ideas differently and see different patterns emerge over time does not mean that any organization of an idea is acceptable. When students organize ideas in ways that do not seem to make sense, they need to be challenged to reflect on and justify their reasons, and they may need to modify their work accordingly or be pressed to understand a gap in reasoning. In this example, if I had put wine in the breakfast category, I would have to justify that by admitting to a drinking problem—or a critical-thinking problem!

When asking students for justifications, however, I would like to offer a piece of advice based on my experience. In many cases, the connections students see, especially gifted and highly creative students, can be highly sophisticated and nuanced—far beyond what you might expect. What at first may seem random may actually be incredibly astute. Listen carefully to their wildest responses because they may present chances to expand learning and push all students to think deeply in a way that fits into the natural flow of a lesson.

When we stop asking students for rote answers and stop spoon-feeding information in tidy, bite-size pieces, they begin to look for sound reasons to justify their thinking. Teaching students how to visualize the content of a debate provides clues about where to look for evidence and how to structure a persuasive argument. By adding the responsibility of evidence-based argument to the learner's plate, we transform learners from recipients of information to brokers of ideas.

This brings us to our next reflection. What kind of cognitive activity is happening in the Organize phase of the Webstorm? Organizing, especially at the beginning of the process, seems simple, but it is actually a wonderfully complex process that engages the whole mind. Our left hemisphere seeks to find order in the visual chaos by coalescing ideas logically in groups; it starts by finding two nodes that go together and building outward. This sequential thinking shows the part-to-whole nature of left-hemispheric thinking and exemplifies convergent thinking. The whole-to-part thinking of the visual right hemisphere has a different, yet complementary role. It can see a big picture and find many intuitive ways to synthesize the whole idea by working inward and finding patterns in the randomly displayed information.

Seeing groups by looking at the bubbles and grouping them into categories demonstrates *understanding of the vocabulary and content*. However, organizing goes beyond understanding. It requires analysis. Students need to analyze and evaluate information to group it. Is a particular item a breakfast food or a dinner food? Is it a grain or dairy? This analysis gets more complex the more deeply we look at our symbols. Is pizza a grain? I had a slice of pepperoni and a slice of veggie.

Which group should it go into? Each slice of pizza has cheese (dairy), tomato sauce (vegetable), and crust (grain), and some have pepperoni (meat). Those are all the food groups right there. This type of reflection and probing analysis exemplifies critical thinking, but is absent in many class discussions.

While I was visiting a middle school and watching a lesson on nutrition, I saw students group fried chicken in the meats group. Later, I asked the teacher about this decision, because it seemed like a natural time to bring up the concept that foods can belong to more than one group. He replied that this would be too much for the students, and that they were better off with hard-and-fast rules. On one level, I understood his point; strict rules are easier to understand. However, I was dissatisfied with this outcome and felt that we had shortchanged our students, or at least denied them a more nimble understanding of the topic. After considering the point further, I've concluded that this type of attitude can cause more serious damage. If students believe that the world works according to exact and inflexible rules and that answers are already known, then there is little hope of discovering better ways to solve problems and little motivation to find new answers. They will be left confused when patterns don't fit, and yet will have few strategies to help them handle nuanced information.

As educators, we are challenged to spur critical thinking and increase rigor, and visual strategies like the Webstorm encourage students to see the complexity of the world they live in and to grapple with the questions they face. We do not need to shy away from complexity; rather, we need to offer students tools that help support a more sophisticated understanding of the world. Our students will surprise us. Would they have come up with a "processed food" category? Would they have grouped by calories? Could this activity lead students to an appreciation of the idea that foods, once they've been processed or prepared, often don't fit neatly into a single food group? We should not underestimate our students' ability to digest complicated or contradictory information. We need to provide them with frameworks and strategies to make sense of it. If we do so, they will become independent learners and problem solvers capable of wrestling with the compromises and complexities demanded by the world in which we live.

Several school principals with whom I have worked have told me, "I don't see critical thinking in the classrooms," and many teachers have told me that they are unsure what critical thinking really looks like. I empathize with them because, as a classroom teacher, I asked kids a lot of questions, but I was never quite sure what they were learning from those open-ended discussions. As in all classes, some students dominated conversations, others took lots of notes, some were quiet, and then there were those who seemed miles away. It was very hard to know who was engaged in a discussion and to what degree they were learning.

When student dialogue is represented visually, as we are modeling in this Webstorm, it engages the whole class in visual and auditory modalities. The teacher is put in a natural role of facilitator and high-tech scribe, able to use the interactive visualization as a springboard for asking open-ended questions. The Webstorm makes it natural for teachers to remember to ask students critical-thinking questions like, "Why do you think so?," "How do you think that relates?," and "What led you to that connection?" As students see an idea transform and move around on the screen in concert with the classroom dialogue, all students benefit from the conversation grounded in visual representation. The result of this multi-modal interaction breaks down barriers to learning and invites everyone to participate, either actively in conversation or actively in observation or internal reflection. This process embodies the role of teacher as facilitator and puts the task of thinking squarely on the shoulders of students.

Step 3: Write Subtopics

After the content is organized into groups, the visualization is made up of piles of nodes, each containing a similar type of information. The net effect is a rough approximation of how the idea fits together. The next step in the process is to **Write subtopics**. Creating the subtopics represents another burst of analytical thinking that is augmented by visual inquiry. This step requires Webstormers to look at the content critically and make decisions about how to label the groups.

Completing this step goes a long way toward evolving the brainstorm into a cohesive web. The process of identifying and adding subtopics forges the direction an idea takes and focuses the content. The technical steps in this process are simple, but the thinking involved can be quite challenging because it may reveal inconsistencies and outliers that don't seem to fit. Reconciling the information will require some cognitive heavy lifting. Fortunately, the ability to physically move pieces and evaluate them visually facilitates the process.

When the idea is partially resolved—meaning that at least one or more subtopics are established and aligned logically with supporting details—it is common to experience a noticeable lull in energy because of the mental effort involved in grouping ideas. At this point, it may be time to skip forward to Step 4 and Link. Some toggling back and forth between the Organize, Write subtopics, and Link steps is natural and productive.

For this Webstorm, I wrote the subtopics in two different ways, to exemplify how different groups may attack the challenge. The first example depicts a scenario in which the class organized the material into two groups and in this step wrote in two subtopics (fig. 7.6).

The second version shows a scenario in which the class organized the idea differently (fig. 7.7). The students wrote four subtopics because they categorized their brainstorm using food groups. The second version contains a few nodes that don't fit perfectly into the groups—a very common occurrence reflecting real-world scenarios that are not black-and-white. As a teacher, it can be disconcerting to have to reconcile information that does not have a tidy bow tied around it. In truth, however, you should embrace this scenario. Outliers and incongruence

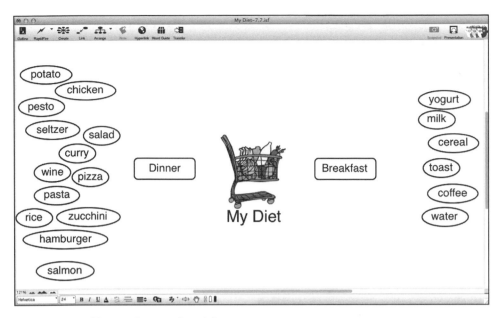

FIGURE 7.6. Emerging web with two groups.

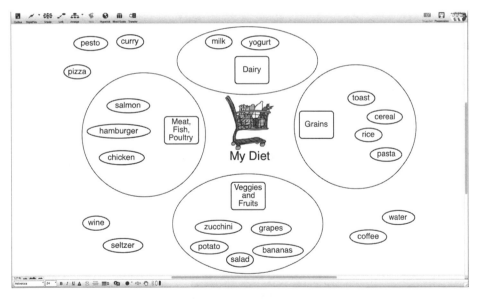

FIGURE 7.7. Emerging web showing outliers.

present valuable opportunities for discussion, dialogue, and decisions, all hallmarks of higher-order thinking.

In this example, the items that don't fit into groups can be considered "outliers." As a teacher, you should view the presence of outliers as a superb opportunity to facilitate a rich discussion about how to refine the idea. Here are some questions that spur critical thinking about the categories in an idea and can help to resolve outlying nodes:

- Should the subtopics be broadened to include the outliers?
- Should subtopics be more specific?
- Do the subtopics relate to one another and hold the idea together?
- Should the outliers be deleted because they don't fit the topic?
- What would happen to our idea if we made these changes?

In coaching the Webstorm, I emphasize that conversations have their own sequence but that not all of the information contributes to the topic. In fact, it would be rare for all ideas within a given topic to fit together cleanly and be completely on point. Some ideas may be valuable but go beyond the scope of the task. Others may miss the mark. (Half of the material I have edited from this book fits into that latter category.) Helping students embrace the fact that they can delete and revise are two of the greatest higher-order thinking skills we can teach!

The procedure for completing this step is as follows:

1. Prompt your students to look critically at the groups they created during the Organize step. Ask them to think about how they would label each group.
2. Ask students to identify what those labels should be. I use a few different prompts to facilitate this step, such as, "What would you name this group?," "How would you label this?," and "If those details were all in a drawer, how would you label that drawer?" These questions tend to work for me, but I encourage you to create your own. Note that this step requires teacher wait time. For clear categories, this step will go quickly, but if there is debate over how to best label a group, this activity can take a while, and the labeling may be a source of lively debate.

3. Add a new unlinked node that provides the label for the group. Position the new symbol between the details and the main topic. In the first example, "Dinner" and "Breakfast" are the two labels.

4. If possible (depending on the tool being used to Webstorm), change the color or shape of the subtopics to set them apart from the rest of the map. If you are using paper and pens for your Webstorm, create a visually distinct treatment for the nodes that are to be subtopics.

Help students embrace the fact that they can delete and revise— these are two of the greatest higher-order thinking skills we can teach!

Writing the subtopics is a critical phase of the Webstorm process and should not be rushed. Below are a few guidelines to ensure that this phase of the process is successful and meaningful.

Tip 1: DO NOT provide students with the subtopics. DO NOT assume you know what will emerge. The teacher who chooses the subtopics will have stolen a rare and wonderful opportunity for students to think critically, justify their thoughts, and develop their analytical skills. Determining the subtopics, like organizing the items into groups, is higher-order thinking that engages your students and promotes thoughtful and insightful class discussion. Be on your toes in your role as teacher/facilitator. What your students come up with may surprise you.

Tip 2: Sometimes one of the existing nodes may actually be the best label for that group. This occurs when someone has added that node during the Brainstorm phase. When this happens, simply drag the node from the pile into the proper position between the main topic and the details.

Interpretation and Analysis

Once you've written the subtopics, reflect on the energy level in the class during this phase. Did some students seem energized as they searched for the best word to describe a group? Did some find the process overwhelming and tune out? Take note of how student engagement changes depending on whether you are Webstorming a tangible idea—such as food or a sequence of events—versus abstract concepts like freedom or courage.

As the concepts you work with while Webstorming become more complex, some students will experience mental fatigue sooner than others and at different parts of the process. Other students will not engage until the concepts are more sophisticated and worthy of debate or analysis. Watch the general ebb and flow of student and class energy during this process. At different times, students will disengage and reengage, depending on their mental saturation, personal tendencies, and interest in the topic. The Webstorm process allows students the chance to see ideas develop, consider them holistically, and digest information at their own pace.

Step 4: Link

Visual magic starts to happen when nodes are **Linked** together. This energizing process is fast and easy. In a flash, Webstormers see their work transformed into a cohesive idea because linking the nodes reveals the first real iteration of the web. Regardless of the tool used to Webstorm, adding the links formally establishes the conceptual hierarchy of the visual outline. Even though the layout of the subtopics visually and spatially suggests relationships, until links are established, all nodes are technically Level 1 nodes. Once nodes are linked, their hierarchical levels are established. Links also decrease the visual complexity of a diagram, so linking one area of a map helps students regain the mental energy to revisit the Webstorm and focus on other areas within the diagram that may still need to be resolved. In figure 7.8

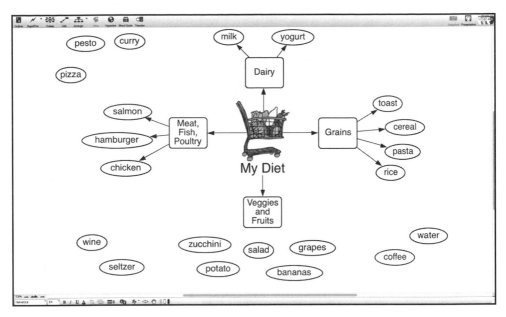

FIGURE 7.8. Linking ideas.

links transform the image from a sea of bubbles into a relatively cohesive idea in progress.

Notice that many of the nodes in figure 7.8 are not yet linked. It is not necessary to link the entire diagram in one fell swoop. Organizing the content of an idea (Step 2) and deciding on subtopics (Step 3) are both mentally taxing processes. Linking is an energizer that recharges the brain by simplifying the diagram. Before the idea was linked, it was made up of about twenty-five separate nodes. The first phase of linking reduced the number of floating nodes to twelve. For the working memory, cutting information in half is akin to a splash of cold water to the face: it refreshes the mind and enables a new wave of visual inquiry.

The time to link is *when the class starts to lose energy or momentum from organizing or writing subtopics.* Any branch can be linked as soon as it has a subtopic and some details. Usually, the first area ready to be linked is the one with the most tangible information. The last ideas to be resolved are generally more abstract. Moving nimbly back and forth between linking and writing subtopics at the onset of the inevitable energy lull will yield outsized rewards. Much-needed mental rest and visual clarity will come and will lay the groundwork for productive, efficient critical thinking.

Outliers, as I mentioned earlier, present a challenge and an opportunity to visual organization. The next web below makes it easy to see outliers (fig. 7. 9). Pizza, pesto, curry, wine, seltzer, water, and coffee do not fit in with the subtopic labels. It was difficult to think of categories that would encompass that information and still make sense in the overall representation of the idea. Working out how to resolve outliers can stump a group and will slow the momentum of the activity.

This quagmire has a simple solution. For the time being, *leave them there*! This is the precise time to shift gears to the Link step. As we link what seems clear, the idea settles visually into a more comfortable form. Instead of trying to reconcile a concept that has a sea of unlinked nodes, linking lets the group focus on the few outliers that need to be resolved. Outliers teach us a lot.

1. **Outliers foster questions that require critical thinking and lead to deep understanding.** These outliers can guide you, the teacher,

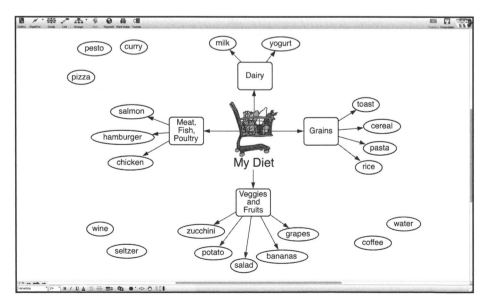

FIGURE 7.9. Web with outliers.

to ask probing questions that cause students to dig deeply into the subject matter. You can easily generalize questions based on this principle for any subject matter. The outliers in this example should suggest the following questions:

- Why don't these ideas fit in? Why doesn't pizza fit? Is it a grain, vegetable, or dairy? Is it a combination of all three?
- Is there another label we should add? Like drinks? Does another label make our idea clearer? Does a new label improve what we are trying to convey? What other foods do you eat that might not fit into these categories? (Fried chicken? Lasagna? Spaghetti and meatballs? Sandwiches?)
- What do these foods have in common? (They are cooked with foods from other groups; they contain ingredients from other groups.)
- When do foods fit most easily into the food groups? (Before they are processed.)

These questions require students to analyze, reflect, evaluate, predict, and use evidence. All these tasks promote the kind of learning that helps students become independent thinkers.

2. **Outliers focus learners on the scope of the topic and encourage students to delete, delete, delete.** Have you ever taught a student who consistently chose topics far too broad or too general to be suitable for the assignment? This is a common problem, especially for the highly creative divergent thinkers who tend to go on tangents and who struggle to turn their ideas into cohesive and structured works. By seeing ideas spread out too far, they can understand when they are going astray. Learning to see when to delete also helps overachieving perfectionists who attempt to develop ideas that go far beyond the intended scope of the assignment. Not that we want to limit effort or creativity, but sometimes

the hardest-working students need the most help keeping a project in the proper scope.

Deleting is a challenging lesson for students. Many of them hate it because it feels like going backward—it requires them to remove work they have done. After the Organize and Write subtopics, and Link steps are underway, students will often try *too hard* to make all of the bubbles fit into categories. This is a mistake because it breaks the logic of the idea. Outliers should be allowed to hang there in space to give students a chance to take their time and process whether the idea is necessary and needs to be integrated or whether it is a tangent that breaks the flow of the argument.

Deleting outliers requires complex thinking and does not happen quickly. Speed is not the objective here. This activity is nothing like doing times tables or any other act of rote memory or recall. When we present students with complicated decisions, we need to honor that complexity by giving them time to wrestle with the mental demands of original thinking. Our more introverted and thoughtful learners, in particular, will welcome the chance to contemplate and reason instead of deferring their classroom contributions to the extroverts who race to blurt out answers.

When students delete, they learn to identify what belongs in their idea and what does not. Deleting is one of the most essential critical-thinking skills we can teach students, and in doing so, we teach them to refine their ideas from diamonds in the rough into the gems they can be.

3. **Outliers serve as placeholders.** A valuable role of outliers is that of "idea placeholder." One of the most effective aspects of the Webstorm process is that it accommodates divergent thinking in a completely fluid manner. If your students have a hunch that an outlier might be relevant later, keep it off to the side of your web, unlinked, for possible future use. If it finds a home in the idea

later, then it will be ready to be used. Alternatively, if the outlier placeholder never quite fits, it can always be deleted.

For highly creative and nonlinear thinkers, people with ADHD, visual-spatial-oriented learners, and anyone for whom ideas are plentiful and often distracting, the placeholder node provides an urgently needed strategy for keeping wild facts and mildly related notions at hand. For this population, the Webstorm offers a strategy that accommodates unrestrained creativity while providing a structure that makes it clear how to refocus on areas that need to be addressed.

Interpretation and Analysis

Linking allows the mind to rest, recharge, and refuel. It also provides Webstormers with a newly refined and developed version of the web that significantly ratchets forward the visualization of the idea. The previous steps have been cognitively taxing, even if they have not always felt difficult. The lower-order-thinking act of recall yielded the initial content. This phase is productive while participants have sufficient cognitive fuel to perform recall. The process of grouping and sorting, as we demonstrated, is an act of critical thinking and decision making. Once the mind gets tired, as the cognitive load fills to capacity, the linking phase can bring closure and produce a simple visualization that ties together the prior work. Linking makes it easier to see where the idea stands, and it allows the Webstormers to recharge their mental batteries so they can address outliers and embrace the next round of the process.

As you embark on the Link step of the Webstorm, take note of the energy of your class. Compare this energy level to that of the Organize phase. Does it feel calmer? Do students express a sense of satisfaction from completing a task? Is there an ease that permeates the class? Did you feel an intellectual burst while ideas were generated, followed by a sense of calm as they were linked together? I hope you did. This has been my experience Webstorming with students and teachers, and for my own purposes.

Congratulations! You have just completed the first phase of the BOWL and LADLE process for completing a Webstorm. In the next phase, we will use the LADLE to stir the idea and refine the concept into a four-star cognitive first course that prepares the idea to become a hearty meal.

CHAPTER 8

Stirring the Webstorm: Using the LADLE and Making SOUP

The BOWL gets an idea out of the mind and into a workable format where it begins to take shape. The next phase of the Webstorm process—the LADLE—takes a second pass at the idea to develop it further. The LADLE is made up of five components: **Look, Add, Delete, Link, Evaluate**. These are not, however, rigid, sequential, steps. They represent a holistic, inherently flexible visual approach to working with ideas.

The LADLE is not as dramatic as the BOWL, when the ingredients were first added and the idea began to take form rapidly. The LADLE is more like stirring the broth, around and around, processing the idea until it is smooth and clear. The LADLE builds on all of the critical thinking done earlier. With its cognitive load refreshed after a vigorous first round of visual thinking, the mind is ready to go further with the idea and hone any aspects that need more work. Webstorming is an iterative process. There is no limit to the number of times you can stir the LADLE. It is a time to methodically work through the idea until the visualization is complete. In this second round of visual inquiry, the concept will become fully developed and take a form that can serve as a basis for any future task that is required.

After using the BOWL and LADLE method to Webstorm, the third phase of the process has to be called SOUP. Once the idea is fully developed as a web, it can be used to develop **Slideshows,** draft **OUtlines,** or write **Papers or project plans, or to prepare for a test.** For students, this may also include planning a script or storyboard or delivering an oral presentation. For teachers, Webstorming may become the preferred method for designing instructional units and planning lessons. It certainly is for me. Regardless of the end goal, the BOWL and LADLE process makes a high-quality outcome easier to achieve.

PHASE 2: LADLE

Look Add Delete Link Evaluate

Step 1: Look

Look at the web that represents the current state of the idea. Observe what you have. Take it in holistically. Acclimate yourself to your idea and be open to new waves of recall or discovery. Take stock of what fits well and what does not. As you look at your web, ask new questions to advance your idea:

- Which areas are fully developed?
- Are any ideas underdeveloped?
- Are there obvious gaps that I need to address?
- Does anything I see spark new ideas?
- What should I do with the outliers?
- Do my logic and organization make sense?

- Does my web have visual balance?
- Can I do anything to make it more visually meaningful?

This holistic approach to evaluating the idea is the essence of visual inquiry, and it is a metacognitive strategy. When looking at your idea, your eyes tell you a lot about what needs to be developed and provide clues for how to proceed.

Step 2: Add New Information

After looking at the "My Diet" web, I realized I could include more. I added new details to all Level 2 nodes. When you lead a Webstorm activity in the classroom, students will see things to add in this revision because they interacted with the material so thoroughly during the BOWL. That active, multisensory experience developed content schema and provided a framework on which to build new information. The space between nodes (what artists would call negative space), the position of nodes on the screen, and their colors and shapes all help students generate new ideas to add.

Traditional lists and outlines, in contrast, are linear, not spatial. They only allow the learner to work with an idea as a vertical sequence. Lists and outlines provide neither visual clues to help one see gaps in logic, nor do they provide a flexible framework to generate new ideas. In contrast, the image that follows (fig. 8.1) shows how simple and easy revision is in a Webstorm. The LADLE explicitly asks learners to Add new nodes to the web. Students will intuitively use both convergent and divergent thinking in this process. In some cases, existing nodes will trigger the next logical expansion of that topic. In other cases, an idea could trigger another idea that sparks a completely new way of analyzing the main concept being considered. (Additions in this iteration, figure 8.1, are indicated with a bold outline.)

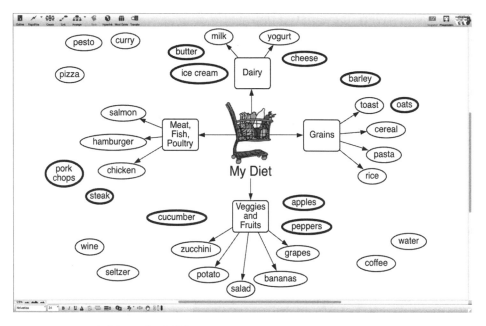

FIGURE 8.1. Add to the Webstorm.

Step 3: Delete

Deleting details is a valuable critical-thinking exercise. When students analyze their webs and find that items on them do not integrate with their subtopics, they may decide to delete them. Students learn a valuable lesson when they acknowledge that, just because they added an idea to a web does not mean that it should make the final cut.

By encouraging students to prune extraneous details from the web, you will help them focus on answering the question being asked. All teachers have had the experience of a student who took on way too much—far more than was asked—and whose work suffered because of it. This step teaches students how to make decisions and work within parameters, in addition to giving them valuable academic and professional skills essential for time management and productivity.

> By encouraging students to prune extraneous details from the web, you will help them focus on answering the question being asked.

Step 4: Link New Items

The web below shows the new items (with bold border) that were **Added** and **Linked** during the LADLE process (fig. 8.2). In general, fewer outliers will be added in the LADLE process, because the structure and organization of the idea will have already been established in the BOWL. Linking in the LADLE phase can happen any time new nodes are added to the web.

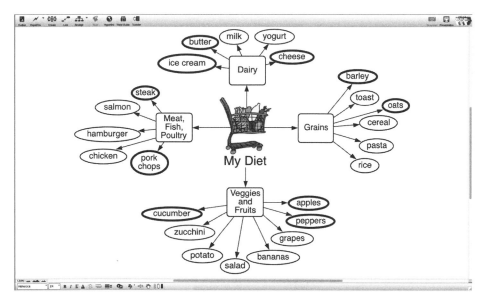

FIGURE 8.2. Link nodes added in the LADLE.

Step 5: Evaluate the Web

Does the web communicate what you want it to? Does it represent the idea as well as it can? Does it have a logic and flow? Is there more to Add, Delete, or Link? For many students, a second pass through an idea using the LADLE process will be sufficient and will provide a comfortable place to finish a Webstorm. Others will need to "stir with the LADLE" a few more times to refine the organization or content.

When an idea is pretty well "cooked," students may want to further revise the web by adding images or changing aesthetic choices. These modifications are engaging and more than merely decorative. They strengthen comprehension by putting visual hooks into the idea. Students tend to select images that match their associations with the objects, which enhances recall and long-term memory. Even color, link style, and visual embellishments like font size can add meaning to a web.

The **Evaluate** step in the LADLE focuses on critique and assessment, though evaluation actually happens at every step of the Webstorm. Evaluation through visual inquiry of the diagram is an opportunity for students to revisit their concept, make creative breakthroughs in understanding, gain new insights, find new pathways to explore, and efficiently restructure the idea in a way that satisfies the requirements of the activity and the learners' intellectual curiosity. The teacher has a central role in the Evaluate step to challenge students to question their logic and dig deeply into their thinking. Here are a few thought-provoking questions that teachers can ask students to help them evaluate their ideas:

- How well does this web represent our topic? Why?
- Does it answer the question?
- Are there aspects of the topic that the web does not address? What questions does it lead you to ask?
- What are your thoughts on the outliers? Why were they hard to categorize?
- Did the outliers suggest other questions to explore about the topic in the future? If so, what?
- What changes would occur in the overall representation of our diet if we simply deleted the outliers? Would the web still answer the question?
- If the outliers are essential, how can we modify the web to account for them in a meaningful way?
- If the outliers don't fit in our web, where should they go? They are still a part of our diet.

Interpretation and Analysis: There is always a temptation to "solve" the outlier problem by adding a "Miscellaneous" category. This is *never* an acceptable solution. "Miscellaneous" is a cop-out category. If your students *want* to add "Miscellaneous," they *need* to stir the LADLE again. A well-constructed web cannot include this category.

It is possible that the Evaluate step will lead to a completely different representation of the idea, with different subtopics and a different overall message. This is the case in figure 8.3, which shows Evaluation in progress. In a new round of Adding, students expanded their concept. They considered that "Drinks" was a good category to add. They also noticed that the four food groups contained only single-ingredient items, and were generally raw. Through questioning and reflection, a student realized that "hamburger," formerly in the "Meat, Fish, Poultry" group, did not fit neatly because it could fall into at least two categories.

Debate ensued. Students noticed that a hamburger contains grains, possibly cheese, and sometimes vegetables. All told, it was a complicated scenario. They were beginning to grasp a critical concept: nutrition is complicated. As debate continued, they realized that some foods that seemed healthy at first—like fried chicken—may in fact not be so healthy because of the way they are processed, or because of ingredients that are cooked with them.

Through Evaluation, the visual inquiry process led to debate, critical thinking, and finally to deeper understanding. The process allowed students to construct a more flexible, nuanced interpretation of nutrition. This new, more realistic visualization represents the type of learning that can impact students' lives today, by giving them tools to make informed daily dietary decisions, and tomorrow, by giving them the tools to take on sophisticated critical-thinking endeavors.

Revising the web to reflect this new understanding is not simple, because the topic is complex. It would require significant reorganizing and possibly a completely new envisioning. Because the pieces are in front of us to see, however, the process is more like putting together a puzzle than totally reformulating an idea.

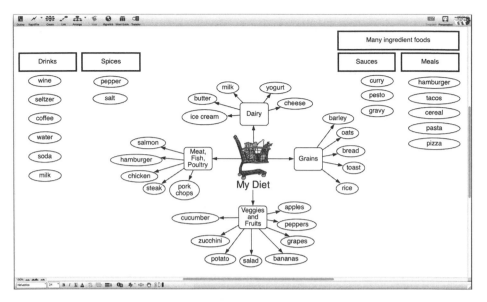

FIGURE 8.3. Evaluation and re-envisioning in progress.

In a final iteration of this activity, this sophisticated visualization of "My Diet" shows a strong grasp of diet and how foods are interrelated (fig. 8.4). It is the product of many rounds of critical thinking, observation, discovery, and reflection. As teachers, we strive for metacognition, and the BOWL and LADLE process places the onus of critical thinking squarely on the shoulders of students. By "stirring the LADLE" as the idea simmers, students analyze their webs, evaluate their content, and, finally, create the web that represents a flexible understanding of the topic.

Take a moment to study this Webstorm. Observe the detail and digest the volume of thoughtful, logical, rich content that is represented. Count the words and symbols that it took to represent this concept, and think for a moment how much student understanding this map reflects. Consider how useful it could be for myriad academic tasks.

- If this were the visual aid for an oral presentation, how detailed and informative could the presentation be?

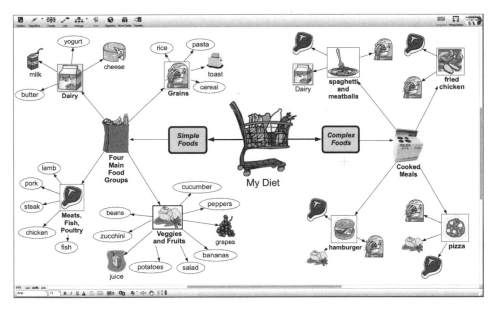

FIGURE 8.4. Complete Webstorm created through the BOWL and LADLE process.

- If this web were to serve as a graphic organizer for an essay, how well structured and organized would that essay be? How much quality writing would it generate?
- If this web were to serve as a tool for test preparation, how well could students transfer this information?

Imagine your students' enthusiasm as they share their thoughts and the intellectual confidence they will gain by learning to visualize complex ideas.

What Have We Accomplished with the BOWL and LADLE?

The BOWL and LADLE is a process that we need to teach students in order to prepare them to think critically. It is a powerful strategy that is easy to do and it accomplishes many of the objectives of effective teaching. Just a few of the virtues of the BOWL and LADLE include its ability to:

- Create a student-centered classroom
- Position the teacher as facilitator and co-learner
- Differentiate instruction by providing an alternative way to represent and work with information
- Expand the capacity of working memory and cognitive load
- Activate prior knowledge and provide a framework for assimilating new knowledge
- Provide an explicit process for inquiry and critical thinking
- Encourage thoughtful student-to-student interaction and effective speaking and listening

The versatile Webstorm engages the creative, associative parts of the mind to visualize an idea and the linear, logical parts to help structure it. This process leverages our innate human ability to group, sort, and see relationships and fit new information into our personal schema. The Webstorm serves us well as a skill for a lifetime of teaching and learning. Whether the final form of an idea is a movie, a paper, a debate, or a presentation, the skill of cooking up a well-developed, organized idea is the central skill for success. With mastery of the BOWL and LADLE process, our students will be empowered to turn their ideas into any kind of SOUP that they can possibly imagine.

PHASE 3: SOUP

Slideshows OUtlines Papers, project plans, preparation for tests

Who doesn't love SOUP? Whether warm or cold, clear or creamy, soup can have a hundred different textures and ingredients. All good SOUP, however, requires a well-executed recipe. The third phase of the

Webstorm serves as a reminder that organization and planning are the most important ingredients for any consistently successful outcome. Before you get the SOUP, you need to do the prep. Jumping into any project without a plan is just a bad idea.

Phase 3 of the Webstorm is called SOUP because it is an ideal way to accomplish the planning phase for any academic project, regardless of the final form that deliverable may ultimately take.

- Webstorming is perfect for preparing a slideshow-style presentation (PowerPoint, Keynote, Google Slides, Haiku Deck, etc.) because it allows the learner to separate the tasks of developing content and message from the task of formatting slides and adding embellishments such as transitions.
- Webstorming is a better approach to outlining because while webs are, in fact, visual outlines and they engage more cognitive tools to organize an idea than traditional outlining.
- Whether the product is a paper, proposal, paragraph, podcast, parody, play, plan, or preparation for a test, the Webstorm process will provide the proper piquancy.

Slideshows from the Webstorm

Slideshows and presentations of all kinds benefit from a Webstorm because the process allows students to organize the content before becoming distracted with the features, formatting options, evil transitions, and horrid sound effects that tend to enrapture them. For teachers concerned with content and exasperated with spinning checkerboards, asking students to develop ideas first as webs will lead to improvement in organization and more robust substance. It will also eliminate the tendency for students to write sentences into slides, which is a bad practice that should be extinguished. Because webbing uses *one idea per node*, it will eliminate sentences from slideshows, encourage students to "speak to" the content on their slides, and reduce the tendency for them to simply read them.

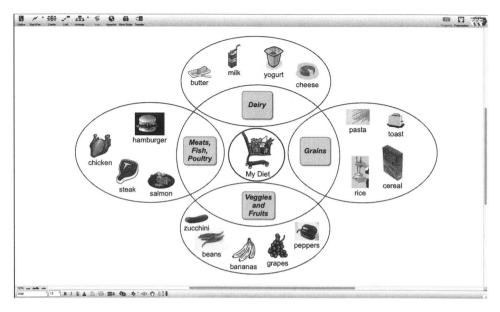

FIGURE 8.5. Correlation between web and slideshow.

The hierarchical content structure of webs lends them to linear slideshow presentations because the organizational structures match. Figures 8.5 and 8.6 demonstrate the correlation between a web and a slideshow taken from the "My Diet" example (fig. 8.5).

It is easy to see this relationship. The Level 1 main topic of the web becomes the title slide of the presentation. The subtopics from Level 2 nodes become the body of the second slide, serving as a table of contents for information to come. Then slides three through six show the details that are represented in Level 3 of the web.

Take a few moments to reflect on the potential of this relationship. In most PowerPoint, Keynote, and Google Slide projects, students spend most of their time on formatting and layout—and a fraction of their time on the content. This is the wrong emphasis, but webbing changes that equation. It gives students a place to develop their ideas in a format conducive to thinking and learning, instead of wasting precious time with bells and whistles.

The powerful relationship between web and slideshow was not lost on software companies. Some webbing software tools, like Inspiration

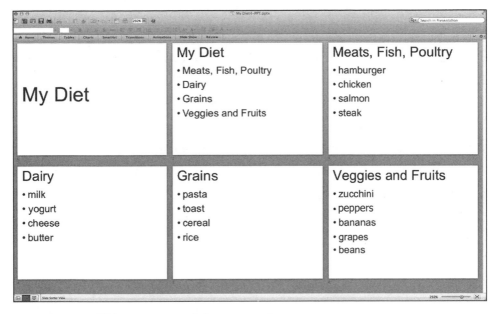

FIGURE 8.6. Slides generated from a web.

and Mindjet, enable an unbelievably convenient feature: direct export from web to PowerPoint. Other mind-mapping tools, such as iMind-Map, have a "play" feature that creates an animation that flows from one node to another, zooming in to each part of the web, in an order that the user can define. Prezi is not specifically a webbing or mind-mapping tool, but it fits into this family of innovative presentation tools that provides a more dynamic viewing experience for the participant. Even if the webbing tool used for planning a presentation (i.e., pencil and paper) cannot automatically export to PowerPoint and the user needs to retype text on slides, by creating the web first, the process of researching and organizing is exactly where it should be—at the beginning.

As an instructional technologist and educator, I maintain a pretty strong position against slideshows as "default" student projects because students spend more time fiddling with features than focusing on content. Student slideshows are even more wasteful when precious class time evaporates while students read their slides to their teachers while classmates snooze, drift, or use the time to mentally practice their own presentations. Regrettably, this model is still common. (For an infinitely superior method, search "dyadic belt" in your favorite web browser, or contact me and ask. This is an old favorite oral presentation strategy from my days as a Spanish teacher.)

I hold an even stronger position against slideshows as teaching tools because they put students in the role of passive recipients of information. Slideshows present information in bite-size, ordered chunks. The only learning task that students can do with a slideshow is to remember what was on the slide. Recall is lower-order thinking, at the bottom rung of Bloom's Revised Taxonomy. Slideshows are also time-consuming to create. Teachers can easily spend hours making them, considering carefully how to convey the information clearly. What a meaningful learning experience *teachers* reap through this process! Not so for students, who usually only get to watch and listen. Well-intentioned teachers get a rich learning experience by synthesizing information, and they inadvertently steal the higher-order thinking from their students in the process. How ironic is that? (Brief disclaimer: thoughtfully designed instruction—of which slideshows may be a part—can naturally be highly beneficial learning experiences.)

For a reliable and effective way to teach content that has students doing the thinking, try a Reverse Mind Map (see chapter 9). It will be a class-saver and a time-saver—and it may transform your teaching practice. You may never make a PowerPoint again.

Outlining from the Webstorm

The web–outline relationship that we first explored in chapter 5 is one of the key attributes of visual thinking. Teachers have been asking students for outlines since pencils were invented for a simple reason: because they work. Outlines help in test preparation. They offer a road map for organized writing. Outlines also provide a standard structure for contracts, proposals, and research. There is no dispute about the merits of outlines, but they're not easy to create.

People don't usually think as sequentially as an outline requires, as demonstrated in the proof of nonlinear thinking in chapter 4. That example illustrated that, because of the pattern-seeking nature of our minds, we often think in the surprisingly nonlinear order of 1–3–2 (main topic, detail, subtopic). However natural this order is for thinking, when we need to write a paper, make a presentation, or complete another sequential task, we are better served when we use the linear order of an outline, which is 1–2–3 (main topic, subtopic, detail). The ability to arrive at a linear outline from a nonlinear webbing exercise is a powerful outcome with practical implications.

> However natural nonlinear thinking may be, when we need to write a paper or make a presentation, we are better served when we use the linear order of an outline. Fortunately, arriving at an outline from a web is much easier than creating an outline from scratch.

Arriving at an outline from a web or mind map is much easier than creating one from scratch. Outlines oblige a rigid form of sequential thinking that requires the learner to drill down within each subtopic to add and order subordinate details before proceeding to the next subtopic and repeating the process. In contrast, maps allow learners to develop ideas by level (thinking about all of the Level 2s, then all of the Level 3s, etc.), which helps develop parallel organization. This is often easier than thinking about each detail within a subtopic before moving on.

The transition from web to outline, however, is a step that warrants a little attention, because there is no inherent order of subtopics in a web, though there is in an outline. Outlines show hierarchy by vertical order (top to bottom) *and* horizontal order (indentation). Webs only show hierarchy by level of each node. In some cases, students will need some support in making decisions about the priority of subtopics and details within subtopics when they move from the web phase to the outline phase. This evolution is natural in the development of an idea.

In the "My Diet" example used to show the Webstorm process, the order of the subtopics was not very important, but for many topics it is. For topics that have a chronological or linear sequence, like essays and summaries, suggesting to students that they arrange subtopics clockwise around the center node of the web is helpful. Even in our digital age, in which fewer people wear analog watches, people seem to *have schemas for clockwise orientation* that transitions well to webbing. In other cases, ideas that have a linear quality may be better developed using a tree diagram, because top-down tree diagrams have an inherent left-to-right and top-to-bottom structure that visually aligns well with the sequence of an outline.

Students will generally create webs with a composition that enhances the visual literacy of their ideas. If not, review the principles for evaluating ideas visually in chapter 6. A few of the best tools that enable simultaneous webbing and outlining—Inspiration and Kidspiration (software) and Inspiration Maps and Idea Flip (iPad apps)—allow the user to look at the topic in either web or outline view. In outline view, they allow users to promote and demote topics simply by dragging and dropping items within the software. The web and outline are two distinct ways to work with the same idea, and both have tremendous utility, depending on learners' needs at a given time.

Papers, Project Plans, Preparation for Tests

There are many academic tasks that start with the letter *p* that the Webstorm process can support (as well as tasks that begin with the other twenty-five letters of the alphabet). Following are a few examples of webbing strategies to help students in writing papers, working on projects, and preparing for tests. Chapter 11 provides many more examples of visual strategies, but to emphasize the versatility of the Webstorm process for diverse academic tasks, this chapter concludes with a few examples to ensure that our SOUP has enough flavor.

Papers are some of the most challenging assignments for students because writing is among the most difficult of academic skills. Using the Webstorm to create a writing plan or starting from a template makes the process visual and provides a roadmap for the task. Many types of essays and arguments can be constructed visually. One approach to mapping out a comparison essay is shown in figure 8.7.[1]

Project plans are useful for students who struggle to manage their time and complete long-term, multi-faceted projects. A project plan

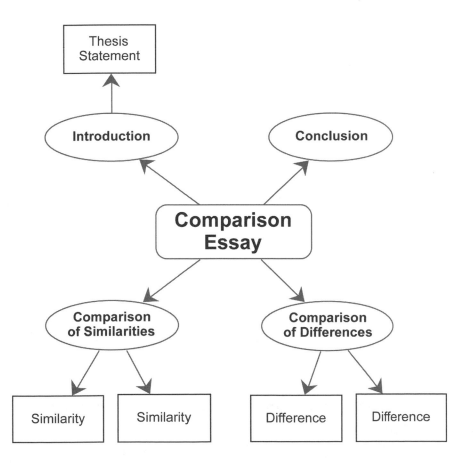

FIGURE 8.7. Comparison essay web.

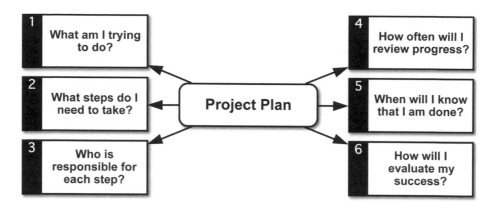

FIGURE 8.8. Project plan.

web lets students see how the components of a project contribute to the whole, and it provides them with a way to move forward when they are stuck. In many cases, students who can see the framework of their project can be coached to skip to a part that they can do and return to the tricky spots later. This nonlinear approach helps students to keep progressing on ideas once they realize that they do not have to work in a set order from start to finish (fig. 8.8).[2]

The study plan template is another way for students to take ownership of their learning (fig. 8.9). To prepare for a test, students can use a web to predict the topics they will need to study. By looking at a picture of all the resources they can use, students will be empowered to take ownership of their learning.

As an additional benefit, this nonlinear approach allows students to progress through tasks in any order and remain productive. A study plan helps students manage their progress and persevere because they can see the light at the end of the tunnel. Without a plan of attack, the prospect of studying can be overwhelming and may lead students to give up. A study plan not only helps them reach short-term goals like academic achievement, it also teaches them how to be independent lifetime learners and responsible professionals.

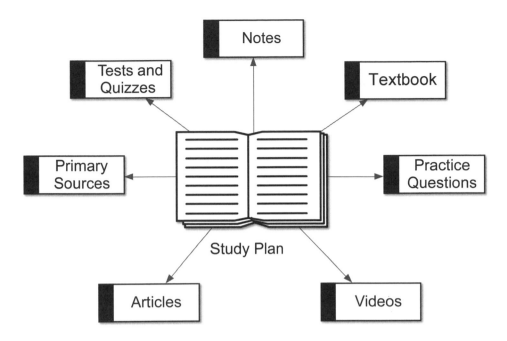

FIGURE 8.9. Study plan.

Closing Thoughts on Webstorming with the BOWL and LADLE Process

My promise in this book is to deliver a step-by-step, go-to strategy that helps individuals or groups start with the kernel of an idea and develop it into a format that can take any shape. As an educator and someone prone to divergent, right-hemispheric thinking, I know firsthand how badly such a strategy is needed. But before I explicitly identified the steps of visual thinking, I never knew that it is as much a convergent thinking strategy as it is a divergent one. Visual learning may be a term popularized for a certain type of learner, but the process illustrated in these chapters works for anyone. The BOWL and LADLE is a method that all learners can use to problem-solve, reason, and communicate ideas clearly. The Webstorm is a versatile outcome of this replicable procedure that can be a cornerstone of your teaching practice.

I hope I have made visual thinking seem easy to do, and I sincerely hope that I have motivated you to try this method. Most importantly, however, I call upon you to teach the Webstorm strategy to your students. Emphasize that it is a strategy for *learning, planning, and doing anything.* It is a tool they should put in their back pocket and take with them to college, graduate school, and any trade or profession. The more diverse places you integrate this method, the more convinced you will become of its universality, and the deeper you will drive this point home. Help your students gain experience with the Webstorm and the BOWL and LADLE process so that their standard plan of attack for any questions and challenges they face is to picture their ideas with diagrams and webs. With your help, visual thinking can become a weapon of mass achievement!

CHAPTER 9

The Grand Slam of Visual Thinking: Webstorm, Reverse Mind Map, Summary Man, and Constructed Response Magic

Our deep dive into the BOWL and LADLE process laid a foundation for effective visual thinking and provided a framework for discovering new ways to teach and learn diverse topics and skills. This chapter continues down that path by providing four grand-slam strategies that have immediate impact in the classroom: Webstorm, Reverse Mind Map, Summary Man, and Constructed Response Magic (which consists of the Puzzle Prompt and the Web Prompt methods). These strategies can be used with virtually any subject matter and targeted to any grade level.

Webstorm is included in this section in a distilled version, not to explain the BOWL and LADLE process again, but to model a more sophisticated topic and to demonstrate how the process can be integrated throughout a unit of study. **Reverse Mind Map** is a variation that never fails to generate thoughtful student dialogue and critical thinking.

Summary Man models how webbing can serve as a mnemonic device that exists only in the mind's eye. **Puzzle Prompt** is a two-part strategy that provides our first foray into visual inquiry as a method of deconstructing text for reading comprehension and explains how to use that deconstruction as a prewriting strategy. Puzzle Prompt has direct application to the constructed-response requirements so common in today's standardized testing environment, though it has implications far beyond that for note taking and active listening.

The Webstorm

The **Webstorm** uses the BOWL and LADLE process explored in depth in chapters 7 and 8 as a framework for teaching an instructional unit. The Webstorm is perfect to:

- Introduce or pre-teach a lesson or unit, because it reveals what students know about a topic
- Use as the hub of an instructional unit because it can evolve as a living document that the class builds throughout the unit, revealing what students have learned and how information fits together
- Use as a study guide and as an assessment tool
- Use to differentiate and individualize instruction

Teaching the Webstorm

The Webstorm is ideal as a stand-alone lesson or as the hub of an entire unit that holds together everything covered from pre-teaching to summative assessment. In the example that follows we will look at how to use the Webstorm as a hub for a unit on the Civil War.

Sample Plan for Civil War Webstorm Unit

Essential Questions

Why did the Civil War happen?

What is the long-term influence of the Civil War on the United States today?

Learning Standard(s)

Common Core: W.4.8. Recall relevant information from experiences or gather relevant information from print and digital sources; take notes and categorize information, and provide a list of sources. (Other standards apply.)

Learning Goal(s)

Students will be able to complete Webstorm activities to respond to the essential questions.

Materials and Accommodations

Computers (laptop or desktop) or tablets

Digital projector

Interactive whiteboard

Visual thinking software or app

Paper, markers, tape, chalk/dry-erase board (if technology is not available)

Although interactive whiteboards and computers can enhance this strategy, it can be done effectively with paper, pencils, dry-erase boards, or other low-tech or no-tech teaching resources. Schools have different classroom resources, so even if you do not have this technology, think about the big idea of the Webstorm, and adapt it using what you have. For instance, students could write responses on loose-leaf paper that could be taped to the wall or positioned on the floor to be moved as necessary, in ways that follow the model of the lesson. Teachers have always been resourceful, so do what you need to in order to capture the spirit and thinking involved in this activity, even if it is done low-tech.

Activity Sequence/Method

Day 1: Formative assessment
Day 2: Explore gaps
Day 3: Debate
Day 4: Compare then with now
Day 5: Summative assessment

Day 1: Formative Assessment: BOWL

On Day 1, teachers can conduct a formative assessment by completing a Webstorm activity using the BOWL and LADLE process. In the sample that follows, this formative assessment is treated as a whole-class activity. The teacher is the facilitator, prompting the students with questions. She is also the scribe, adding items to the screen. Students in a class with one device per student could do this individually. Figures 9.1 and 9.2 show the use of the Webstorm for this purpose, and the procedure is described below.

1. Launch visual thinking software or prepare alternative materials.
2. Add a central node and name it "Civil War." This will be the main idea, your Level 1 concept in your web. Display so that students can see the topic clearly.
3. Prompt students: "In this unit, we are going to learn about one of the most important periods of American history and explore whether the issues that it dealt with are still issues today. Today is the first day of our study. To begin with, we are going to see what we already know about the Civil War."
4. Follow the BOWL and LADLE procedure.

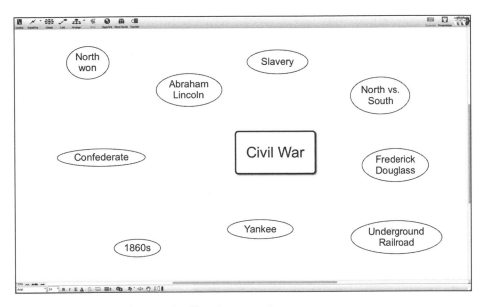

FIGURE 9.1. Initial round of brainstorming.

BOWL: Brainstorm, Organize, Write Subtopics, Link

After one round of brainstorming in a pre-assessment Webstorm activity, students may not reveal a lot of prior knowledge of the topic. Their responses may resemble the ones above. While these responses show a limited level of understanding, they are the seeds of our idea and show the place to begin learning. After some prompting in the BOWL, even this basic level of knowledge will expand. It also takes time for students to remember what they actually know on a topic. (The Organize, Write subtopics, and Link steps of the BOWL are not pictured because they evolve like the example in chapter 7.)

LADLE: Look, Add, Delete, Link, Evaluate

A second round of work on this web, completed in the LADLE phase, yields a more thorough formative assessment of what students know about the unit (fig. 9.2). Any gaps in prior knowledge provide a road-map of areas to emphasize. This image shows the final result of work that followed the Look, Add, Delete, Link, Evaluate procedure.

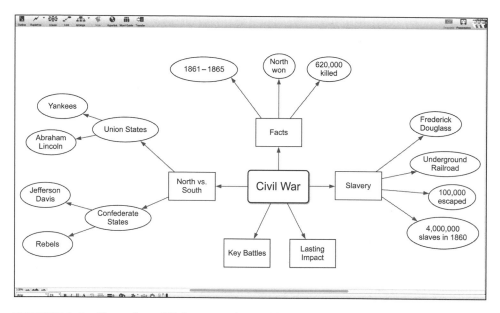

FIGURE 9.2. Complete Webstorm formative assessment using BOWL and LADLE process.

The Webstorm now shows a broader knowledge of the topic than was shown during the BOWL, and it provides a direction to proceed in the days to come. This early iteration shows the teacher and students that "Key Battles" and "Lasting Impact" are two areas that will be explored.

Days 2–5: Explore Gaps, Debate, Compare Then with Now, Summative Assessment

The pre-assessment Webstorm will reveal gaps in understanding and therefore prescribe possible areas for study. The teacher may use Day 2 to explore "Key Battles" or the "Lasting Impact" of the war. Perhaps the teacher will choose to use the original Webstorm as an opportunity to present other gaps that need to be explored, for instance, "Factors Leading to War." There are countless ways to use the Webstorm as a springboard to build on the original snapshot of student knowledge provided by the formative assessment. During a unit of study, the Webstorm can and should spur questions to be explored through studying interactive maps (with tools like Google Earth), analyzing original documents, watching and discussing videos, and by debating states' rights versus national rights in small groups. Students can address different areas within the scope of the unit through group projects and report back to the whole class. There are countless ways to engage students in authentically meaningful work to expand their knowledge of a topic, but the Webstorm serves as the hub that holds together all of the unit's components.

> A pre-assessment Webstorm will reveal gaps in understanding and therefore prescribe possible areas for study.

Every day, each new facet of learning should be added to the original web. This is a terrific way to begin and close a class. By the end of a unit, the Webstorm will have evolved into a map of everything that was studied. It can reflect every website visited, every video watched, every skit presented, every class discussion, every book chapter read, and every primary source that was analyzed. In figure 9.3, the web grew from the first day to reflect "Factors Leading to War," which serves as a natural contrast to "Long-term Impact." This contrast provided lively debate that students saw as still relevant today, also reflected in the web.

The importance of building on gaps in knowledge that students discover for themselves is not to be underestimated. Curious learners are infinitely more engaged when they see for themselves what they don't know. By the end of the unit, a Webstorm will have evolved to reflect new learning and a deeper understanding of the topic. It can serve as a study guide and as documentation for the journey of learning that students took to arrive at its completion.

When classes culminate by adding the day's new material to the unit web, students are clear about what they have learned because they see for themselves exactly what they have accomplished that day.

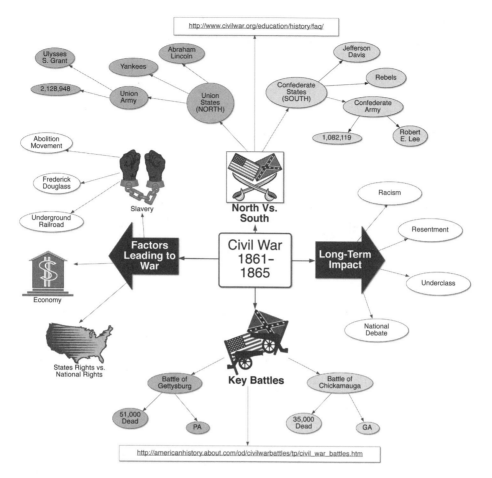

FIGURE 9.3. A web can be a learning hub that evolves throughout the duration of a study unit.

Assessment with the Webstorm

To maximize the impact of the Webstorm, this activity (which began as a pre-assessment) can naturally evolve every day and be used to monitor progress. Information can be added to it after each reading and related activity, so that by the end of the study, days or weeks later, the web documents all of the related areas of study and provides a summary of the entire unit.

The Webstorm offers many assessment opportunities. During the unit, for ongoing formative assessment, students should return to the original document and add new learning to that original Webstorm, as a daily continuation of the LADLE process. Consistent and repeated reflection on prior and current learning will provide multiple touch points with the material to generate a level of enduring understanding that cannot occur when information is taught once or twice and is not assimilated well.

Another type of formative assessment, possibly designed as an *exit ticket* or a *check for understanding strategy*, is to ask students to respond individually to a topical question in the form of a web. This assessment places an emphasis on conveying detailed content understanding rather than producing a few rote sentences beginning with "Today I learned that…" Because webs are quick to create and show a lot of information in a distilled format, they provide teachers with a more thorough window into student understanding.

As a summative assessment, teachers could ask students to create their own representation of the topics of the unit, speak to a particular area of the web, or write a written response to some aspect of the web. The only summative assessment that *I would not recommend* is to ask students to fill in a blank version of the Webstorm that was created through the unit. This task would serve to test recall rather than assess more complex thinking on the topic. Asking for a fill-in-the-blank web misses a terrific opportunity for students to demonstrate the depth of their knowledge and their mastery of the content.

The Webstorm process should not be drawn out or laborious. It should be energetic and engaging. Webstorming doesn't even necessarily need to culminate in a fully developed web. It can simply get students engrossed and primed to start learning about the topic. It can be integrated as a prereading activity or a visual support to class discussion, group work, writing, or a project. Any topic that warrants a classroom discussion warrants a Webstorm because it provides a meaningful and lasting representation of a class dialogue that engages students and allows them to see how an idea fits together. It facilitates new learning and connections with other topics. There is no limit to the versatility of the Webstorm, and a few areas to explore include:

- Historical events
- Scientific processes and cycles
- Essay planning (descriptive, persuasive, informative)
- Test preparation
- Compare and contrast exercises
- Characterization
- Summarization
- Vocabulary acquisition
- Classification

The Reverse Mind Map

The **Reverse Mind Map** is one of the fastest, most engaging, and most effective visual thinking strategies that exist. Plus, it is incredibly easy for teachers to prepare. The Reverse Mind Map is closely related to the Webstorm, but in contrast to the Webstorm (which starts as a blank screen with one central idea), the Reverse Mind Map shows all of the necessary puzzle pieces on the screen from the start. To prepare a Reverse Mind Map activity, the teacher will complete the **Brainstorm** and **Write the subtopics** steps of the BOWL and LADLE process prior to class and then scramble them on the screen for students to **Organize** and **Link**.

This activity is called a Reverse Mind Map because, in contrast to a traditional mind map that grows outward from the center node, the Reverse Mind Map *starts with only floating nodes*. Then, through student dialogue and discussion, it evolves into a mind map in a nonlinear fashion, based on the way students recognize patterns in the information and choose to assemble that information. The Reverse Mind Map follows the 1–3–2 (Main topic→Detail→Subtopic) pattern recognition sequence that is so natural to critical thinking.

The challenge of the Reverse Mind Map is for students to put the idea together, not to recall all of the content. Because the Reverse Mind Map shows all of the nodes of the idea on the screen from the start, the emphasis for student learning is not on recall but on analysis and evaluation of content. Students benefit by looking at the floating nodes on the screen, which serve to jog their memory and activate prior knowledge. The nodes also help students recognize patterns by providing clues to relationships in the information. These factors directly support working memory and enable students to effectively use visual inquiry to assess and group information. The Reverse Mind Map is perfect for teachers looking to:

- Assess student knowledge of a topic
- Engage the whole class in exploring a topic
- Gain experience and expertise facilitating class discussions in the role of guide and co-learner
- Infuse critical thinking in discussions
- Create a student-centered learning environment
- Eliminate the need to present information through PowerPoint

> Because the Reverse Mind Map shows all of the pieces of the idea from the start, the emphasis for student learning is not on recall but on analysis and evaluation of content.

The Reverse Mind Map is a fast-paced activity that gets everyone involved in critical thinking immediately, because the first thing students are asked to do is find patterns in the information and organize it in groups. This approach is ideal for introducing ideas or as an assessment strategy. Like a Webstorm, a Reverse Mind Map can serve as a hub in a unit, or it can be a way to close a lesson to reinforce the content covered in class.

Sample Plan for World War II Reverse Mind Map Activity

Essential Questions
What was World War II and why did it happen?
What is the long-term influence of World War II and why is it important to the United States?

Learning Standard(s)
Common Core: CCSS.ELA-Literacy.W.4.1.a. Introduce a topic or text clearly, state an opinion, and create an organizational structure in which related ideas are grouped to support the writer's purpose. (Numerous standards apply.)

Learning Goal
Students will be able to complete a Reverse Mind Map to respond to the essential questions.

Materials and Accommodations
Computers (laptop or desktop) or tablets
Digital projector
Interactive whiteboard
Visual thinking software or app
Paper, markers, tape, chalk/dry-erase board (if technology is not available)

Activity Sequence/Method

First, open your visual thinking software or prepare alternative materials, then:

- Project the Reverse Mind Map activity.
- Prompt students: "In this unit, we are going to learn about _____. This Reverse Mind Map has a lot of the ideas we are going to explore in this unit. Look for any patterns you see in the information. Let's make some groups." This step corresponds to the "Organize" step of the BOWL and LADLE process.
- Proceed to Organize, Write (or locate) subtopics, and Link the idea until an organization begins to emerge. Use and repeat the LADLE process until the map is fully linked.

Step 1: Project the Reverse Mind Map Activity On-Screen

Below is an example of what a teacher would project on-screen to begin the activity.

First, provide students with one to two minutes of silence to observe the image. Students will often be overwhelmed by it at first. Initially, it will be interpreted as chaos and visual noise. *Teacher wait time is essential in this phase*, in order to give students time to read and process the

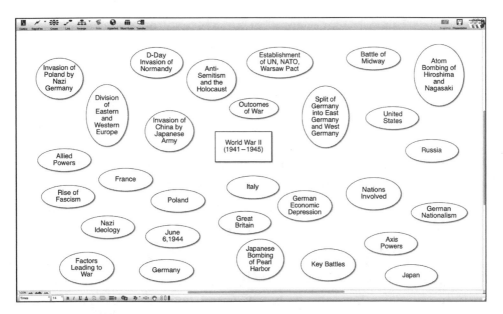

FIGURE 9.4. Beginning of a Reverse Mind Map activity.

words on the map and begin to identify patterns that emerge. The mind is designed to find patterns and rules that make sense out of disorder, so presenting a visual mess is a naturally effective way to draw in students.

After several minutes, ask the students to share the items they think fit into categories. Drag nodes into piles as they provide their responses. *Do not reveal answers or provide an example to follow.* Have patience and wait for students to see the ideas for themselves. They will. Teacher wait time at this key moment provides students with the opportunity to activate a wave of critical thinking that meets the mental demands of the activity. Additionally, by giving students the time to successfully overcome the visual chaos and recognize patterns, they will develop their intellectual confidence and perseverance.

The first time you try a Reverse Mind Map, students unaccustomed to working visually may resist venturing ideas. This resistance is emblematic of a lack of intellectual confidence and inexperience in working through problems that do not have explicitly right and wrong answers. If this occurs, try the prompts below or use prompts from the BOWL and LADLE process (chapters 7 and 8) to get the ball rolling. Ask students:

- Do you see any items here that could be grouped together?
- Can you name two bubbles that you think fit in the same category?
- Can we make any piles of things that go together?

Step 2: Organize the Map

The Reverse Mind Map will take shape as students find patterns and group ideas. As the teacher, group the nodes as the students direct you to. Ask them where on the screen—or the floor or wall if using pen and paper—they want you to drag the items and make the piles. When they identify subtopics, move the subtopic nodes to the Level 2 position, between the main topic and the piles of details. Then go ahead and change their appearance to enhance visual literacy. These steps decrease the visual noise and begin to reveal the emerging idea.

TIP: The class does not need to organize the entire map in one fell swoop. It is likely they will first find patterns and group tangible content, such as places or things, which are easiest to identify and understand. Generally, students will address abstract concepts afterwards. When students show a lull in energy and engagement, their minds are saturated. Respect this energy and use it as a cue to link what they have finished organizing.

Step 3: Link the Map

In this step, the Reverse Mind Map takes shape as students find patterns in the nodes and the teacher links items as directed (Fig 9.5). Students see a progression in their thinking as their web reverse-engineers into an increasingly cohesive visualization of the topic.

The visual noise decreases dramatically after linking begins. This allows students to begin to focus on the more abstract ideas or less familiar concepts of the topic. Continue to evaluate and construct the map as students direct you. When organizing and linking is complete, students will have created a visualization of the concept, transforming the visual chaos they started with into a cohesive, meaningful web.

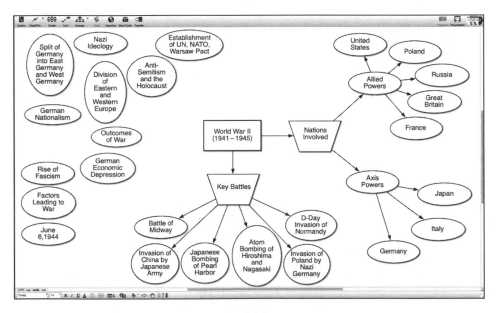

FIGURE 9.5. Linking a Reverse Mind Map.

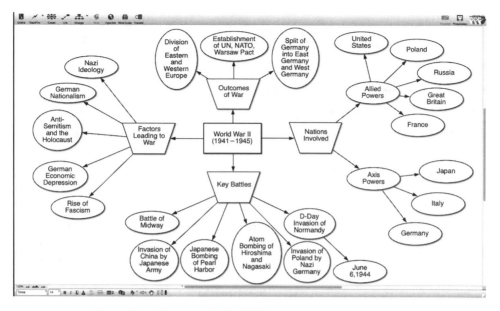

FIGURE 9.6. Complete Reverse Mind Map.

The completed Reverse Mind Map (Fig 9.6) can serve as a unit guide, assessment, or springboard for further study. Try the Reverse Mind Map when introducing any topic of study. Use suggested topics in the Webstorm activity as starters.

Summary Man

Summary Man has a superpower: it scales Bloom's Revised Taxonomy in a single bound while supercharging students' ability to structure and deliver a complete and clear written or oral summary. Do not be lulled by its innocuous exterior. Summary Man taps into the cognitive organization of the human mind by engaging the recognition, strategic, and affective networks as it helps students activate prior knowledge, analyze problems, sequence key events, and predict solutions.

The secret to Summary Man is not vulnerability to Kryptonite. Summary Man has no weaknesses. Its triple-strength learning magic lies in (1) the way the graphic's visual form matches our basic human anatomy,

(2) the fact that it provides placeholders for essential summary questions, and (3) the fact that those placeholders follow the levels of Bloom's Revised Taxonomy from lower-order thinking to higher-order thinking. Summary Man is also an extraordinary visual mnemonic device because it allows students to layer the key components of a summary onto an idea map that visually reminds them of their own bodies (fig. 9.7).

These three factors help students to easily remember and organize content through a seamless process that begins with recall and progresses through the higher-order thinking processes required to draw conclusions and make predictions. Summary Man builds on the schema of the human form as depicted by the stick figures we all drew from the time we were preschoolers. Our deep association with this form makes it simple to co-opt for teaching and learning.

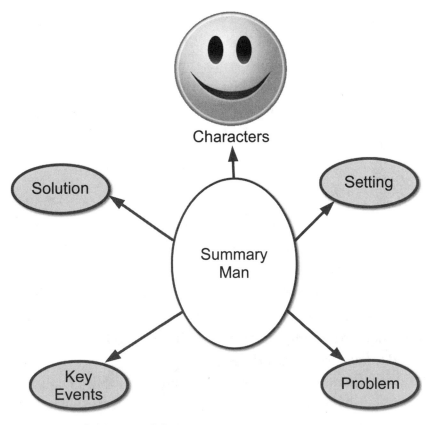

FIGURE 9.7. Summary Man.

Summary Man's head, arms, and legs provide locations for the required information in a summary—characters, setting, problem, key events, and solution. Its smiling face visually prompts students to recall characters first. This is beneficial because the best way to activate prior knowledge is to recall tangible elements of a story. Recall is also the first order of thinking in Bloom's Revised Taxonomy. While it is a lower-order thinking skill, it provides a foundation for analysis, prediction, and synthesis.

"Setting" is also a tangible part of a summary, answering the question "where." It is strategically placed as the next node of the organizer, clockwise from the head. Students have success recalling characters and setting and positioning that information appropriately on the Summary Man web. With students' prior knowledge now activated, they are ready for higher-order thinking and can begin to complete more complex aspects of a summary that require analysis, such as stating the key problem or main idea, sequencing major events, and predicting or analyzing the solution.

Summary Man is simple and a little silly. Students like that. It makes summarizing nonthreatening and more accessible. Whether you are teaching students to write summaries or to summarize orally, Summary Man makes the task easier and improves the outcome.

Teaching with Summary Man for Writing and Speaking

Summary Man is an excellent prewriting activity because it provides a clear way to construct and deliver a response. Once students are comfortable working with Summary Man for writing tasks, this organizer can take on another role, which is to support students in delivering coherent oral summaries. Speaking and listening are essential skills that are finally receiving their due as skills to develop in the Common Core, and Summary Man addresses this need.

Many students struggle to organize and deliver thoughtful and substantive oral responses in class. Several factors can contribute to this skill deficit. Some students don't know how to begin or conclude an oral response. Others have anxiety about public speaking. Still others are hesitant to speak when unsure of their answer. Summary Man can help students build speaking skills because this graphic organizer can be quickly visualized in the mind's eye and provides a framework to guide a student through a response. Examples of Summary Man for written and oral summaries are modeled in the pages that follow.

Sample Plan for Summary Man Written Response Activity

Essential Questions
How can the innocence of children sometimes reveal the ignorance of adults?
What is the essence of true friendship?
In what ways can adults be naïve?

Learning Standard(s)
Common Core: RL.6.2. Determine a theme or central idea of a text and analyze in detail its development over the course of the text, including how it emerges and is shaped and refined by specific details; provide an objective summary of the text. (Numerous standards apply.)

Learning Goal
Students will be able to create a Summary Man diagram of *The Boy in the Striped Pajamas* and use that diagram to write a summary of the story that shows understanding of the plot and themes of the story.

Materials and Accommodations
Computers (laptop or desktop) or tablets
Digital projector
Interactive whiteboard
Visual thinking software or app
Paper, markers, tape, chalk/dry-erase board (if no technology is available)

Activity Sequence/Method

Project the Summary Man template using a digital projector or interactive whiteboard. Alternatively, pass students handouts of the Summary Man template or have students create the graphic-organizer template with pen and paper, laptop, or tablet.

- Replace the text "Summary Man" on the belly with the main topic you want students to summarize. In this example, we will change the text to read *The Boy in the Striped Pajamas*.
- Ask students to identify the characters in the story. Create symbols or nodes to reflect their responses.
- Ask students to identify the setting for the story. Add this information to the web.
- Continue clockwise around the web to complete the portions "Problem," "Key Events," and "Solution."

NOTE: Not every summary will have a solution. It may be more relevant to ask students for a prediction about what they think will happen or how the problem might be solved. Literary elements such as moral, themes, or irony may replace "Solution," depending on the learning objective. Open-ended prompts may also be appropriate, such as "How does this relate to events today?" Adjust and change this final node on the template to reflect the best content for the summary.

The Summary Man activity may yield a diagram like the one in figure 9.8. All students benefit from the visual structure of the representation, which is easy to understand and work with. Students who need more time to internalize the discussions benefit from being able to see the full representation of the conversation for the duration of the activity. This stands in stark contrast to group dialogue that is not visualized, in which ideas are fleeting.

Once an idea is represented as a web, it can be used to write or to create another type of final work. The corresponding outline to this Summary Man may be used to prepare an in-depth written summary.

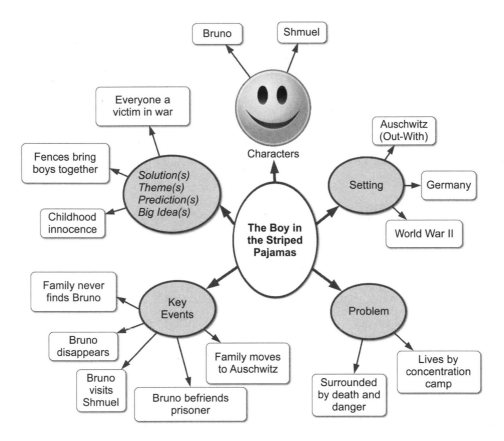

FIGURE 9.8. Summary Man activity.

The Boy in the Striped Pajamas by John Boyne

I. Characters
    A. Bruno
    B. Shmuel
II. Setting
    A. Germany
    B. World War II
    C. Auschwitz (Out-With)
III. Problem
    A. Lives by concentration camp
    B. Surrounded by death and danger

IV. Key Events
    A. Family moves to Auschwitz
    B. Bruno befriends prisoner
    C. Bruno visits Shmuel
    D. Bruno disappears
    E. Family never finds Bruno
V. *Solution(s)/Theme(s)/Prediction(s)/Big Idea(s)*
    A. Fences bring boys together
    B. Everyone a victim in war
    C. Childhood innocence

Sample Plan for Visual Mnemonic Summary Man Activity

It is not always necessary or practical to draw out a summary activity to such a degree. Every day, teachers ask students to summarize a chapter or a concept as a review or as an informal assessment. Summary Man shines as a guide to oral responses for students, especially for those who have trouble organizing their ideas and remembering what they want to say.

To improve oral responses, teach students to recall Summary Man in their mind's eye. Since Summary Man looks like a stick figure, this takes about ten seconds. Then teach them to visualize the information attached to the nodes, and systematically speak to the information that they see in their mind's eye. This strategy is ideal for helping students to start, develop, and conclude concise oral responses to questions.

Oral Summary Question(s)
Please summarize *The Boy in the Striped Pajamas* and conclude with your opinion about the most powerful lesson from the book.

Learning Standard(s)
Common Core: CCSS.ELA-Literacy.SL.5.2. Summarize a written text read aloud or information presented in diverse media and formats, including visually, quantitatively, and orally. (Other standards apply.)

Learning Goal(s)

Students will be able to summarize the story and respond to the question in a coherent and organized oral response.

Materials and Accommodations

Before using Summary Man for oral responses, practice using it for writing. This will assess students' ability to add nodes as details and use Summary Man to systematically progress through a response. Teachers can ensure that students are able to recall Summary Man in their mind's eye by asking them to draw it on paper the first few times they use this strategy. Students should also practice imagining the diagram with details added. Finally, they should practice speaking from Summary Man webs that they have created on paper to make the process of developing spontaneous organized oral responses familiar. Enhancing speaking with visual mnemonics is a tremendous asset for many students, especially as they learn to answer questions and express ideas in sentences, rather than one-word answers. Adding a visual component to help organize such thoughts, albeit an invisible one, will support complex thinking and clear communication.

Activity Sequence/Method

- Prompt students with the question being asked.
- Ask students to imagine Summary Man in their mind's eye.
- Ask students to imagine the details that connect to Summary Man.
- Call on students to answer the question.

Demonstrating an oral process through text may seem a bit stilted, but I will try. Figure 9.9 shows a diagram that would be conjured in the mind's eye. It shows Summary Man and the framework that Summary Man provides on which the student can place the details.

The student's mental image of the filled-in Summary Man provides a "script" to follow, which keeps her on track throughout her response.

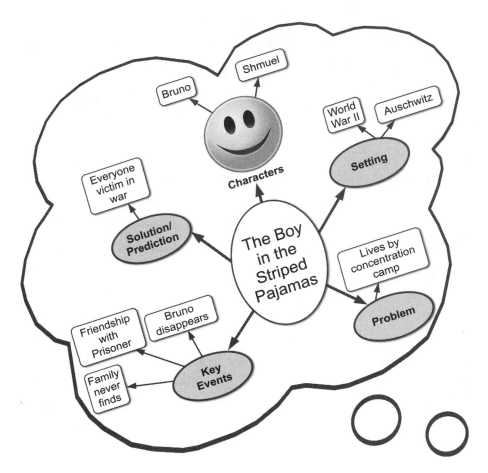

FIGURE 9.9. Summary Man Thought-Bubble Detail.

Using Summary Man makes it easier to keep an idea active in working memory and to speak clearly. Note how the sentences correlate to the nodes in the diagram.

Here is a sample oral response based on the image above:

I enjoyed *The Boy in the Striped Pajamas,* even though it was a sad story. The main characters were two boys named Bruno and Shmuel. The story took place in Germany in World War II. Bruno lived in a big house next to a prison. Shmuel was a prisoner inside it. Bruno made friends with Shmuel. They talked to each other from each side of the fence. One day Bruno snuck under the fence to help Shmuel look for his father. He never got back out and his family never found him. At the end of the book I realized that Bruno was killed in the prison with Shmuel. This story had a big impact on me because of how sad it was. A lot of kids and their parents were killed in the camp. The biggest lesson for me in this story is how everyone suffers badly in a war.

By using Summary Man to visualize a thought, students will harness a sophisticated and powerful speaking strategy that will enhance their ability to respond orally. It will take some practice, but will yield strong results over time. The visualization works so well because it reduces the working memory required for a student to recall and organize all of the content required for the response. Start small with students, asking them to use the method to summarize their weekend or a movie they saw. You will find that Summary Man transforms their ability to summarize in remarkable ways. They will evolve from producing run-on descriptions to delivering concise and fluent summaries with a clear beginning, middle, and end.

Constructed Response Magic

Constructed responses are one of the most common approaches to assessing student reading comprehension and writing mechanics. They are also a heavily weighted component of many states' standardized assessments and are a significant part of Common Core assessments. **Constructed Response Magic** is a two-part learning experience designed to improve student achievement in this high-stakes area. It is helpful for improving standardized test achievement and can be utilized in broader academic contexts too.

Constructed Response Magic Part 1: Puzzle Prompt

Typically, constructed responses require students to read a passage and answer a writing prompt based on that passage. The first step in this process is often to turn the question prompt into a statement. This statement can serve as the topic sentence and focus the writing of the response. **Puzzle Prompt** does this in a unique way by turning the writing prompt into interactive puzzle pieces that students can move around. This interactive process drives home the point that the topic sentence exists within the prompt itself. The Puzzle Prompt should be taught and practiced prior to taking standardized tests and in order to prepare students to answer general written test questions. Once students gain experience with the technique, they should be able to transfer it independently to a testing environment.

> Once students gain experience with the Puzzle Prompt, they can transfer the skill independently to a testing environment.

When teaching the Puzzle Prompt, it is not necessary to read the entire passage with students first. In fact, completing the activity without reading the passage emphasizes for students how much critical information they can glean and use from the prompt itself. In addition, students partially complete their writing in advance and gain a useful filter through which to read the passage. (In my experience, the fact that students do not have to read the passage before doing the Puzzle Prompt has been a huge selling point.)

Sample Plan for Puzzle Prompt

Learning Standard(s)
Common Core: CCSS.ELA-Literacy.W.6.1. Write arguments to support claims with clear reasons and relevant evidence. (Numerous standards apply.)

Learning Goal(s)

- Students will be able to identify the topic sentence of their constructed response from the question being asked.
- Students will be able to rearrange the words of the prompt, like puzzle pieces, and turn the question into a statement.

Materials and Accommodations

Computers (laptop or desktop) or tablets

Digital projector

Interactive whiteboard

Visual thinking software or app

Paper, markers, tape, chalk/dry-erase board (if no technology is available)

Activity Sequence/Method

- Present students with a constructed response writing prompt from a state standardized test from a previous year that has been released for the purpose of study and practice. These can often be found online. Project the prompt onto a screen or interactive whiteboard, or write the prompt on the board.
- Create a Puzzle Prompt with students. Do this by asking students to deconstruct the prompt into words and phrases. The easiest way to do this is to copy the text from an online test booklet, in PDF format, and then create separate interactive words that can be moved around. Figure 9.10 shows a writing prompt deconstructed into a Puzzle Prompt.
- Ask students to create as many valid topic sentences as possible from the prompt by rearranging and removing words as needed. Figs. 9.11 and 9.12 are two possibilities.

Example: Smith Is Gloriously Out of Step

1. Project the writing prompt.

Explain how Smith fits the description of being "gloriously out of step." Use at least three examples from the passage in your explanation. [1]

NOTE: This writing prompt is from a released eleventh grade Pennsylvania System of School Assessment (PSSA) test, which is no longer being used. It is representative of the writing prompts used in Common Core assessments of reading comprehension and writing proficiency. The corresponding reading passage is not shown.

2. Create the Puzzle Prompt.

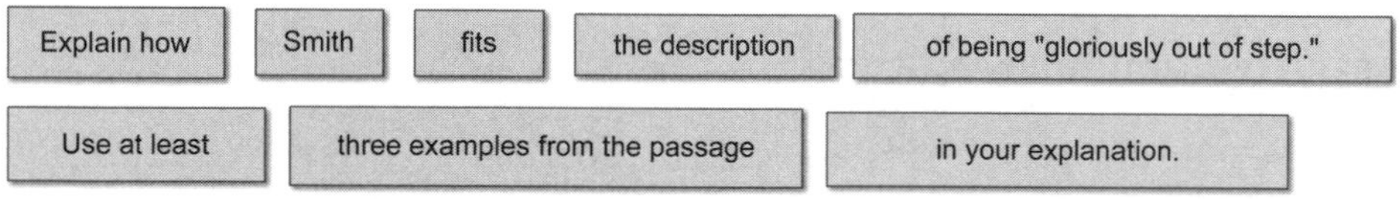

Explain how	Smith	fits	the description	of being "gloriously out of step."

Use at least	three examples from the passage	in your explanation.

FIGURE 9.10. Puzzle Prompt created from the original prompt.

3. Create valid topic sentences.
Answer 1:

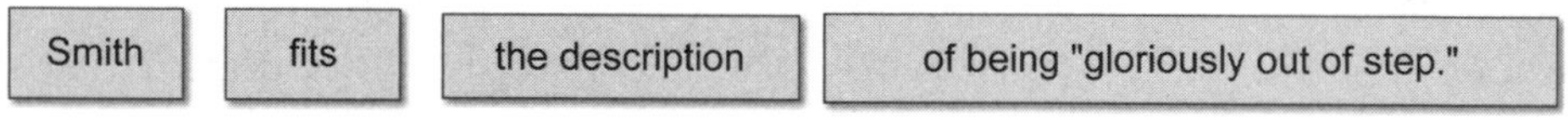

Smith	fits	the description	of being "gloriously out of step."

FIGURE 9.11. One possible topic sentence extracted directly from the writing prompt.

Answer 2:

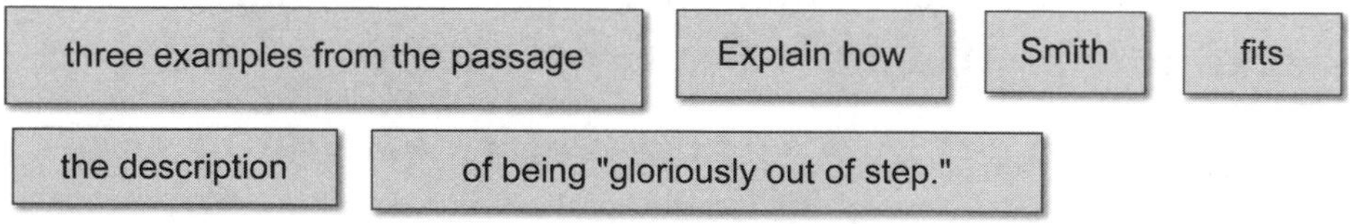

three examples from the passage	Explain how	Smith	fits

the description	of being "gloriously out of step."

FIGURE 9.12. A second possible topic sentence extracted from the writing prompt.

In both of these answers, students dragged words from the projected prompt into a new order that creates valid topic sentences. Some minor editing in the writing process will often be necessary. For instance, some words may need to be altered and punctuation may need to be corrected. As students practice finding topic sentences by reordering words in the prompts, they gain an added benefit of thinking about the passage before they read it. Puzzle Prompt, therefore, serves as a prereading strategy that focuses students' attention on how to approach the passage.

Deconstructing a prompt is a simple and powerful visual thinking strategy that allows a student to find the topic sentence. In Constructed Response Magic Part 2: Web Prompt, students learn to use their Puzzle Prompt topic sentences to create simple webs that further support close reading and effective writing.

Constructed Response Magic Part 2: Web Prompt

The **Web Prompt** is the partner to the Puzzle Prompt. Puzzle Prompt helps students find the topic sentence and Web Prompt helps them develop the rest of the response. Puzzle Prompt provides a useful start to writing. Web Prompt helps focus how students read the passage to find supporting evidence, and it provides a guide to help them write.

A Web Prompt is a quick and clear student-generated web that maps out the requirements of the constructed response question. In my experience, students can learn to create Web Prompts with less than an hour of training and practice. They get the hang of it right away. Students like doing Web Prompts because the webs can be created without reading the passage or writing actual sentences. These are key selling points that teachers can and should leverage shamelessly.

The Web Prompt gives teachers a way of "tricking" students into completing a prereading and prewriting activity, tasks that they are generally loathe to do. This is my big sell: "How would you like to be able to answer the question without reading the passage?" I admit that is a bait and switch because reading is necessary eventually; however,

Web Prompts are quick, easy, and effective. Once students master the skill, they can use this strategy independently when taking any written test. In fact, when students learn to deconstruct language as a web, they gain a skill that can be applied in almost any context, whether academic or professional, for listening, planning, or writing.

The next examples model the relationship of the Web Prompt and Puzzle Prompt to transform students' performance on constructed responses.

Sample Plan for Web Prompt

Learning Standard(s)
Common Core: CCSS.ELA-Literacy.W.6.1. Write arguments to support claims with clear reasons and relevant evidence. (Numerous standards apply.)

Learning Goal (SWBAT)
Students will be able to deconstruct a constructed response prompt and create a web that identifies the information that needs to be answered in the response.

Materials and Accommodations
Pencil or pen and paper
Digital projector

Activity Sequence/Method

- Project the constructed response prompt onto a screen or interactive whiteboard.
- Ask students to create a web with a central node representing the main topic and surrounding linked nodes that represent the facts and justifications required in the question.

NOTE: Words like "three examples" are cues of how to sketch the map, but they are not always the only requirement. In many cases, the question will ask for justification, not merely examples. Students need to read for these nuances and incorporate them into the Web Prompt. After practicing with a few examples, however, students will begin to see the patterns that are shared by many of the questions.

Example 1: Smith Is Gloriously Out of Step

As mentioned earlier, this example is taken from a released item from a former PSSA eleventh grade reading test, which includes written constructed response questions.

1. **Project the writing prompt.**

Explain how Smith fits the description of being "gloriously out of step." Use at least three examples from the passage in your explanation.

2. **Create a Web Prompt that represents the question being asked.**

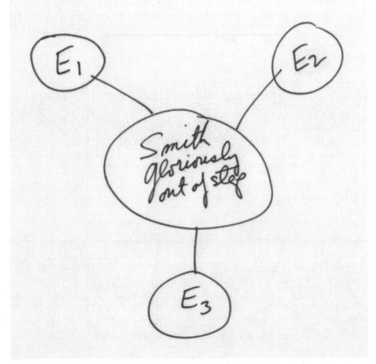

FIGURE 9.13. Web Prompt of constructed response question.

From the writing prompt, students quickly learn to recognize that the main topic of the web needs to be "Smith is gloriously out of step." They then realize that the question is asking for three examples, which they can easily and quickly add to the map (fig. 9.13). Breaking down the prompt into a graphic organizer before reading the passage allows the reader to read purposefully for the information specified in the diagram, to fill in those gaps, and to use the graphic organizer to write. As we see below, using Puzzle Prompt to begin the constructed response gets the student off to a strong start.

Example 2: Space Shuttle Mir

The next example is also from a PSSA writing prompt for eleventh graders. It shows the two strategies (Puzzle Prompt and Web Prompt) being used together. The Puzzle Prompt strategy is used to develop the topic sentence. The Web Prompt strategy is used to create a quick visual plan to help the student read the text for evidence and to write a clear paragraph that fully answers the question being asked.

Writing Prompt:

Identify at least two personality traits displayed by the author. Explain how each trait makes the author a good candidate for the Shuttle-Mir program. Use details from the passage to support your answer.[2]

Puzzle Prompt:

Identify	at least	two personality traits	displayed by the author.
Explain how	each trait	made the author	a good candidate
for the Shuttle-Mir program.	Use details	from the passage	to support your response.

FIGURE 9.14. Setting up the Puzzle Prompt facilitates deconstructing the writing prompt to find the topic.

Puzzle Prompt Answer:

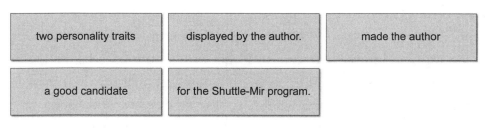

two personality traits	displayed by the author.	made the author
a good candidate	for the Shuttle-Mir program.	

FIGURE 9.15. An acceptable topic sentence extracted from the prompt.

Web Prompt:

The example below visually exemplifies the requirements of the question (fig. 9.16). Web Prompts are usually hand-drawn because students would not have technology to execute this strategy in a normal test-taking environment.

Constructed responses on standardized state tests are the bane of many teachers and students alike. Many teachers dislike teaching this

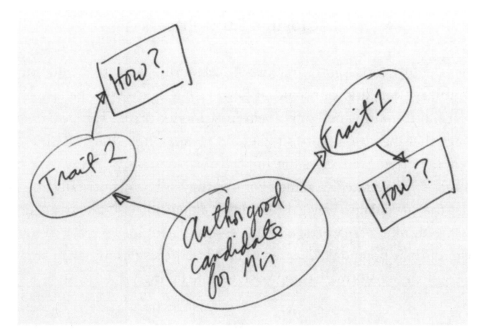

FIGURE 9.16. Web Prompt mapping the requirements of the question.

skill, and virtually all students I have worked with detest writing such responses. Given that predisposition on both sides, I cannot emphasize enough how quickly and easily students pick up the skill of webbing a prompt, and how they seem to forget to hate the process. I surmise that they are so surprised to be taught a strategy that involves sloppily sketching an idea that the whole experience disrupts their schema of this academic experience. These sketches may only take a few seconds to make; however, those few seconds transform the way students read the passage and write their constructed responses.

While skimming, scanning, and closely reading the passage, students can use the Puzzle Prompt and Web Prompt as strategies to capture and organize pertinent information and as a clear way to begin to write. By deconstructing and transforming prompts visually, students can improve their performance on academic tasks like constructed responses, but they can also apply these potent tools beyond the walls of school.

Closing Thoughts

These four grand-slam strategies—Webstorm, Reverse Mind Map, Summary Man, and Constructed Response Magic—take the concepts of visual thinking and apply them in academic areas. The visual language that they use is very similar and it exemplifies the versatility of their underlying principles to impact diverse areas of study. As you embrace these strategies, remember that they are fundamentally guidelines that articulate a way to break down a question or build up an idea. We are thinking creatures, and this series of activities provides only a taste of their potential. Chapter 10 builds on these grand-slam strategies with a transformative approach to note taking.

CHAPTER 10

Transformative Note Taking

Note taking is one of the most tried-and-true facets of teaching and learning, but it needs a major jolt. For decades, elementary, middle, and high school teachers have asked students to take out their notebooks and dutifully write down what is written on the board. I still recall how my high school social studies teacher wrote panel after panel on the chalkboard. We feverishly copied the impeccably structured outlines that Mrs. Bart wrote at an extraordinarily high rate of speed, hoping to finish the task before she erased the board and started again.

We were lucky. Mrs. Bart was an incredible teacher, and most of her pupils and I have her to thank for our ability to take notes and write a five-paragraph essay. In her class we were taught to delve deeply into topics, but what I honestly remember most are those notes—and we wrote scared. Mrs. Bart was old-school and effective. She stated explicit instructions that we knew to follow. For me this meant to copy down everything—which made the monumental task clear, if daunting. Student accountability was never a question because everyone was terrified of her. Admittedly, my memory *may* have exaggerated this account. I have always considered Mrs. Bart to be one of my finest teachers. For me, her effectiveness can be attributed to her no-nonsense, tough-love style, extraordinary subject matter expertise, clarity of instruction, fairness, and high expectations. Most people don't have a Mrs. Bart to model outlining with such vigor and such a tireless chalk hand.

The Problem with Traditional Note Taking

While we were fortunate to have learned these skills from a master teacher, we don't live in the 1980s anymore. Today, Mrs. Bart would be the first to admit that this didactic approach has its limitations. For instance, it may not translate particularly well to other subjects or teaching styles, like working in groups. Nor does it necessarily teach students how to outline or take good notes independently. In addition, more and more classes include diverse media, such as videos and podcasts, as well as texts—requiring students to take notes independently on subject matter that they both see and hear. In some cases, particularly in college classes but also in many high school classes, notes are posted online, so there is little reason for furious note taking.

These changing conditions warrant some reflection about the purpose of note taking. Why do we ask students to take notes? Once we answer that question, we can explore how to teach the skill. Traditionally, the most obvious answer has been that notes document what the class covered and provide a record for future use, like studying for a test. This understanding is still common today. It remains a valid purpose, but it misses transformative learning opportunities. Note taking can also:

1. Engage students in active listening through a multisensory experience that engages the whole mind
2. Provide immediate formative self-assessment that reveals gaps in understanding, thus allowing students to monitor their own learning

The approach most people use to take notes fails to reap these benefits and can even be detrimental to capturing the content. There are many causes for weak note-taking skills. And few teachers know how to teach students this skill. Students are given the instruction to "listen carefully" and write down the "important" words. My interpretation of this instruction (which is shared by almost everyone I have ever asked) was to frantically write everything I heard the teacher say as long as I could keep up. During class lectures, I tried to keep two voices in my head: the teacher's real-time voice and my own inner voice, silently repeating the teacher's words from thirty seconds earlier. I kept half an ear on new information, trying desperately to keep it afloat, while I finished writing down what I had heard just before, at which point I could begin to write down the next wave of information. This vicious cycle continued as long as I could hold onto the two voices. When I lost track, I would stop trying to capture the old information, listen to the real-time lecture to reorient, and start the process again.

This all-too-common approach to note taking presents a serious working memory challenge. To simultaneously listen, remember, and write is just too much to do. Each one of those cognitive acts is complex. Doing them all at once taxes each of the neural networks unsustainably. How can we possibly expect students (or anyone) to actively listen to new material, integrate that content into the body of knowledge they have on the topic, simultaneously distinguish key words that they predict will be useful for remembering the topic in the future, and then write only those "important words" while continuing to listen to new information that keeps coming in?

Schema of the Written Word

A subtle underlying reason why it's so difficult to learn good note taking without a new method stems from the way people think about text on paper. Our schema of text on paper is remarkably well developed, and it is partly to blame for our bad note-taking instincts. For Western language speakers and writers, virtually every text-based experience, from reading books and magazines to writing e-mails and Word documents, includes starting at the top left corner of the page and progressing left to right, top to bottom, until finally the last word in the bottom right corner of the page has been written or read. This is a marvelous convention for written communication, but it presents major challenges for note taking.

People consider note taking an act of writing. When you hand a person a spiral notebook, a loose-leaf binder, or just about any piece of paper to write on, that person will invariably begin to write at the top left corner. We do this because we are trained by years of experience to write just as the text appears in a book. We spend countless hours in school learning to write sentences, not isolated words. We are so hardwired to use text in this manner that we rarely question whether that type of expression is appropriate for taking notes. The transition from writing to note taking is hard because it does not take into account this deeply embedded schema. To take better notes, we need to destroy our schema of text on paper and create a new one that allows our working memory to handle the load of listening, processing, and writing.

> To take better notes, we need to destroy our schema of text on paper and create a new one that allows our working memory to handle the load of listening, processing, and writing.

The Answer Lies in the Fringe
(Fringe Words, That Is)

In chapter 4, we introduced the term **fringe words**. They comprise 20 percent of the words we use in written or oral communication, have clear definitions, and are used in specific circumstances. "Car," "elephant," and "mosaic" are fringe words. As explained, **core words** make up the rest of the words we use to communicate. "I," "why," "on," "for," and "no" are all core words. The radical note-taking method I espouse—no surprise here—is a visual approach that accomplishes the two lofty comprehension and active-engagement goals (listed earlier) and also the pragmatic goal of capturing content that will be necessary to know for the test or paper.

Note taking is really not so much an act of writing as it is an act of representing what we see and hear in a way that we can use later. Visual notes are so effective because the act of creating them obliterates our old schema of what it means to write and replaces it with a new one for capturing ideas diagrammatically with a combination of shapes, arrows, and just a few words. The main casualties will be core words: pronouns, articles, prepositions, adjectives, and adverbs. Verbs will get replaced with arrows. While most of the core words will fall away during note taking in this process (where they are extraneous), they will rise again when our notes become elegant essays or well-articulated responses. By reducing our tendency to write down core words, the text needed to represent ideas can easily drop by 80 percent, yet the meaning is retained because the fringe words are intact. By writing so many fewer words in the visual note-taking process, the learner can capture ideas in the moment. The trick to doing this is to learn how to let the core words drop out of the notes without even thinking about it, and it is easier than you might think.

Our visual notes strategy relies on the creation of webs and mind maps to replace traditional notes—by taking notes in this way, the learner can listen actively and record in real time. This eliminates the need to listen and remember simultaneously. As learners acquire the skill of visualizing ideas, capturing them in webs, and seeing them develop, they gain instant insight into their understanding. The ability to visualize in real time provides the formative self-assessment information they need to ask questions or articulate connections.

Webbing in real time, as a note-taking strategy, engages the whole mind as it processes the aural information it receives. It is a perfect strategy for capturing class lectures, class dialogue, conversations with teachers, or project planning with peers. Learners will be able to apply the principles and execute the steps detailed below to capture this type of information effectively. With this new method of visual note taking, you will naturally stop *writing* notes and learn how to *visualize and map* exactly what you hear.

> As learners acquire the skill of visualizing ideas, capturing them in webs, and seeing them develop, they gain instant insight into their understanding.

Visual notes can be done equally well with pencil and paper or with software. In many cases, pencil and paper are more practical. When the laws of webbing (as detailed in chapter 5) are applied to note taking, visual notes serve as a perfect strategy for active listening and reading comprehension. Visual notes will change the way you and your students listen and learn. The process is simple, though, like anything, it takes practice to master.

How to Take Visual Notes

Taking visual notes is shockingly easy! Here is how you do it:

1. Turn your 8½" x 11" paper sideways (landscape). This simple 90-degree move scrambles your schema of the written page. Notebooks, binders, all other vertically oriented pages are just like pages in a book. Turning the notepaper sideways opens up new possibilities for capturing ideas and will break down the tendency to write unnecessary words. Simply by doing this, you are halfway there.

2. Place the main topic in the middle of the page and draw a circle around it. This further destroys the schema of the text-based page and will incline the learner toward writing single words rather than sentences.

3. Listen for any auditory clues that suggest how to structure the idea as a web. For instance, when the teacher says, "There are three main causes..." the note taker will draw three nodes and anticipate the description of events to follow.

4. Create unlinked floating nodes to capture ideas for which you don't immediately see a logical place. Floating nodes will either find an eventual home in the diagram or will be a cue for the note taker to ask a follow-up question about how that detail relates to the topic.

5. Embellish the diagram with doodles and highlights to create a personal connection to the content.

With the schema of the written page broken, core words will naturally drop out of the note-taking process. Taking these steps will eliminate the tendency to capture sentences, or even core words like "the," which take time to write and simply are not relevant in representing an idea visually. The entire process is liberating. Striking so many words from notes will make it possible to capture ideas fully while actively listening. It gives learners the tools to self-assess, in real-time, their comprehension of the topic.

Finally, and this is important, let yourself go in your note taking. Feel free to listen and doodle or draw. Make circles and lines. Sketch and embellish. Visualize the space that the idea needs to occupy. Fill the page with it. Imagine that the idea can stretch in any direction and allow it to take that shape. Immerse yourself in listening and imagining how that idea grows to fill the space. Let your ears guide your hands. Better yet, let your hands listen. Allow your note taking to be a multisensory experience that engages your ears, hands, and your mind's eye. It will take a leap of faith to trust that you are not crazy when your notes look different from the notes of the person beside you. Embracing your visual mind represents a leap away from the rules about written text that you and your students have spent a lifetime learning. That knowledge and experience are valuable and necessary, but the ability to hear the shape of an idea and capture it visually expands your capacity to listen and learn in an exciting and practical new way. The next few examples model visual notes in different contexts.

Example 1: Visual Notes from Listening

Below are the visual notes I took while listening to Daniel Pink's podcast, "Office Hours," in which he interviewed Twitter co-founder Biz Stone.[1] To begin, I put the main topic in the middle of the page. As I listened, I sketched out the conversation as I saw it unfold in my mind's eye, using the principles of webbing as a framework. When ideas came up that had no clear spot, I jotted them down as floating nodes and figured I'd get to them later. Figure 10.1 is the computer rendition of the map I originally drew on paper.

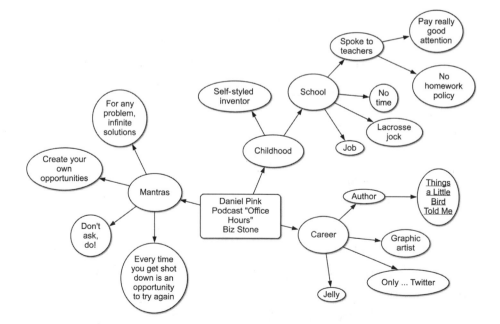

FIGURE 10.1. Notes from Daniel Pink's podcast with Biz Stone.

Example 2: Mapping an Original Idea

I created this second example while I was on a plane to Orlando, in preparation for an iPad workshop (fig. 10.2). Often, I prefer to work with pen and paper because drawing is an intimate, tactile experience that opens up creative pathways. Plus, I get tired of using a computer for everything.

FIGURE 10.2. Hand-drawn workshop plan.

Planning ideas visually is liberating because you do not need to think in a sequential order. By webbing the workshop plan, I was able to work holistically, skipping around the idea in no particular order, but following my intuition and creative process until I was happy with the content and flow of the program. Working in a nonlinear fashion still led to a sequential plan (the idea has a beginning, middle, and end), but the ability to see the entire program develop as a whole ensured cohesiveness.

You can see that the mind map of my workshop plan is not art, though it is visual communication that conveys an idea. No artistic talent is required to mind map. Most people who say they "can't draw" or claim to be inartistic have simply forgotten the joy and freedom of sketching. There is absolutely no requirement to draw mind maps with any precision. Such insecurity is unfounded and counterproductive. Your visual notes are intended for your personal consumption only, so if they make sense to you, they are doing their job.

Example 3: Visual Notes from Text

Taking visual notes improves reading comprehension because it reduces the number of words it takes to document a concept and provides a single picture that holds the idea together. Whether the source is a novel, a textbook, or an online article, these principles apply.

The following example demonstrates the degree to which these factors bolster reading comprehension. A few years ago I heard Wharton professor Mario Moussa speak. I was taken by his ideas and wanted to completely internalize the content of his book, *The Art of Woo*. For me to master a concept takes a herculean effort. As I said before, I am a lousy reader. I constantly lose my place, forget what I am reading, and read inordinately slowly. Conveniently, my desire to master this work coincided with a need to test whether it was possible to map an entire book—the only way I figured I could truly learn the content.

The web in figure 10.3 is the fruit of that effort. It maintains 100 percent of the detail, logic, and examples of the original text. (For the purposes of this book, the very large web is reprinted at a fraction of the scale, which makes the details impossible to read. This is not a problem when creating a web or when viewing the original web on screen.) Sophisticated concepts and vast amounts of information can be expressed in webs. This web is a complete conceptual representation of the book; however, it also lacks something: 99.1 percent of the words.

The book has approximately 110,000 words. The web below has 948. This web is able to represent the full idea with a 1:116 ratio of map words to book words. As first noted in chapter 3, the visual literacy of mind maps and webs is created by their structure, not their words. Symbols and arrows convey the meaning, with symbols representing the nouns and arrows serving the function of verbs. No other parts of speech are necessary. Extreme word conservation is a critical component of the effectiveness of webbing for note taking, because it eliminates the need for a learner to write so many words to create meaning. For both struggling and successful readers, this is a game-changing way to take notes, and it is easy to learn how to do.

In an alternative view of the same web of *Woo*, the central argument is clear to see in a top-level view, which only shows Levels 1 and 2 of

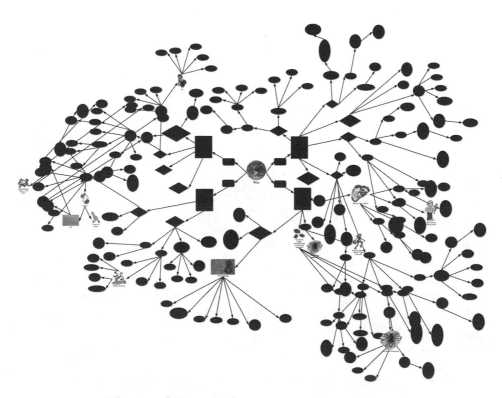

FIGURE 10.3. *The Art of Woo* mind map.

the map (fig 10.4). By deconstructing Moussa's concept to this degree, I could get a handle on it. With this degree of clarity of concept, learning the hidden details below was a simple matter.

The fact that visual note taking can display an idea using only 1 percent of the words of the full text is a radical metric. The implications for struggling readers are immense, but all learners reap an increase in cognitive capacity with a decrease in text. Textbook notes can be reimagined visually by taking cues from the headings, callouts, and other pertinent textual clues. In a program I led at a middle school, students learned the practice of visual note taking using an online article about clouds. Each student personalized his approach to the concept and used image, space, and location to enhance the content and enrich the notes. In all cases, learners were able to eliminate almost all extraneous words from their visual notes and create highly distilled yet comprehensive representations.

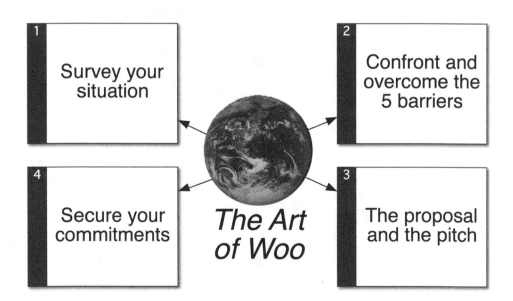

FIGURE 10.4. *The Art of Woo* web showing only the first two levels.

Visual note taking can display an idea using only 1 percent of the words of the full text.

Electronic Notes and E-readers

E-readers like iPads, Android tablets, and Kindles present excellent opportunities for real-time note taking and improved reading comprehension. To assist reading, these devices do a wonderful job of providing features to customize fonts. For note taking, apps have tools for text rendering and defining words. Each device and app are a little different in what they do, but e-reading can often make for more effective reading.

Tablets also enable multitasking, which allows users to toggle between a reading app and a webbing app. Therefore, learners can create visual notes as they read. Toggling is a minimally intrusive step that significantly helps the learner maintain the plot and narrative of a text. This strategy is extremely useful when beginning to read a book in order to get a clear understanding of the characters and how the plot unfolds. With skills in webbing and a firm grasp of how to visualize an idea, users can quickly add details to their map as the narrative proceeds. By reviewing the web before reading or any time the learner is confused or forgets a character, she can use the web to serve as a refresher that activates memory and prepares her for productive, focused reading.

Benefits of Visual Notes

Visual notes transform note taking in two remarkable ways. First, visual notes radically decrease the number of words needed to represent ideas as compared to traditional notes. This amazing accomplishment allows learners to listen to the speaker in the moment and spend less energy scrambling to remember and write what was said. Second, visual notes engage the whole mind in a multisensory learning experience, invoking visualization, the use of spatial relationships, and the act of drawing. In doing so, visual notes reframe our entire schema of the written page and expand our toolkit for capturing and communicating ideas.

These two benefits have numerous positive ramifications. In addition to promoting active listening, visual notes allow learners to see when they don't understand a concept so they can cycle back to the teacher with questions. By mastering visual notes, learners gain immense efficiencies both in terms of eliminating unnecessary words and in conceptualizing the meaning of the content being delivered.

Visual notes offer more than a strategy for the classroom. This form of note taking is useful in the boardroom, meeting room, or even the coffee shop, and it allows listeners to capture the content as an actively engaged participant in academic and professional life. The ability to listen effectively will open doors and opportunities for learners in all contexts. Enjoy, practice, and reap the benefits of this transformative strategy for listening that activates the whole mind.

CHAPTER 11

Visual Classroom Activities

There are many "right ways" to visualize ideas. As long as these ways clearly communicate the idea that they are intended to represent, they are effective. This chapter provides samples of graphic organizers of various types and across diverse subject areas. In some cases, teaching tips and illustrative examples are included. You may draw the conclusion that there is overlap in these examples, even though they are

FIGURE 11.1. Word cloud showing applications for visual thinking.

tailored for different learning objectives. This is intentional. It demonstrates the universality of visual mapping. Ideas drawn as webs, maps, trees, and diagrams can represent many different curricular content areas and can support many different levels of learning.

This chapter is divided into six categories:

- General Webs, Mind Maps, and Diagrams
- Vocabulary, Chronology, and Summary
- Simple Comparison and Analysis
- Complex Comparison and Analysis
- Mapping in Mathematics
- Personal and Professional Planning

These templates and activity starters are intended to enhance your use of visual thinking in your daily classroom practice. Use them as a launching pad to build upon, and adapt them to make them your own. Do not feel limited to using these activities for their stated purposes. Modify them for diverse topics and age groups. Let these activity starters spark your own ideas about how to visualize concepts. Join a vibrant wave of educators in an evolving and creative journey of visual teaching and learning!

To adapt these templates for your own teaching or personal use or to obtain electronic, downloadable files from my website, visit visualleap.com/templates.html, or scan the QR code located in the resources section to open the web page where they can be downloaded.

General Webs, Mind Maps, and Diagrams

Most of the examples and processes we have defined for visual thinking fit under the umbrella of webbing and mind mapping. This makes sense, because semantic webs and mind maps have the unique ability to grow organically to represent both simple and complex ideas. Following are a few we are familiar with, as well as a few other visual ways to think.

Basic Semantic Web

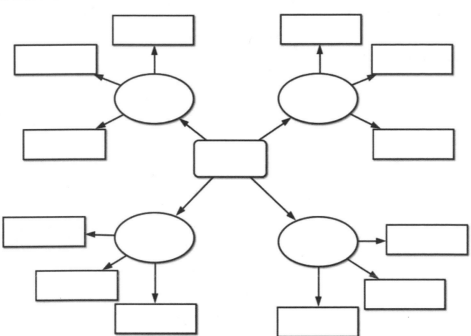

FIGURE 11.2

Basic Mind Map

Use the mind map the same way you would use a semantic web. Try hand drawing mind maps and adorning them with pictures and illustrations that are meaningful to the creator.[1]

A few topics for webbing and mind mapping in the classroom:

Vocabulary
Classification
Characteristics or traits (of anything)
Comparison (i.e., cells, characters, clouds, etc.)
Biography and autobiography
Summary
Word lists

Systems (i.e., body systems, simple machines)
Branches of government
Study guides
Time management analysis (i.e., how you spent your week)
Goals and to-dos
Lesson planning

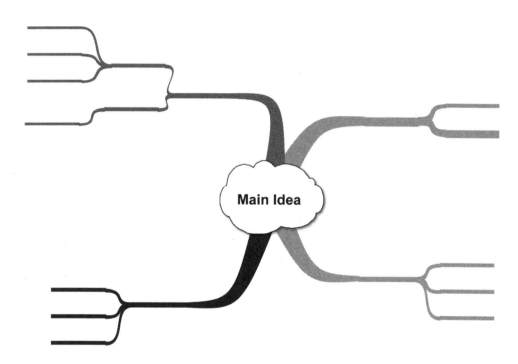

FIGURE 11.3

Basic Venn Diagram

This basic Venn diagram can be used to compare any two categories. Expand the versatile Venn by adding more categories.

A few topics for comparing and contrasting:

Two animals
Two environments
Two games

Two technologies

Two genres

Two events

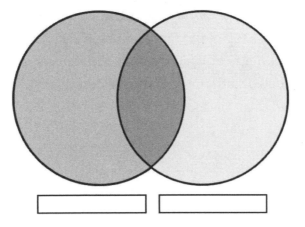

FIGURE 11.4

Basic Flowchart

Use flowcharts to create decision trees that explain processes. Flowcharts are particularly useful to map mathematical and scientific procedures.

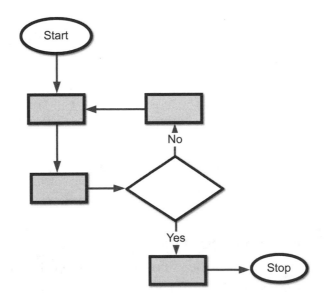

FIGURE 11.5

Basic Concept Map

Concept maps are related to webs and mind maps, but they do not correlate to outlines because of their structure. Concept maps begin with
the main topic at the top of the representation and build down and out-
wards. In concept maps, any nodes can be linked to show relationships,
and links are labeled with the appropriate connecting word. In concept
maps, connected ideas read like sentences.[2]

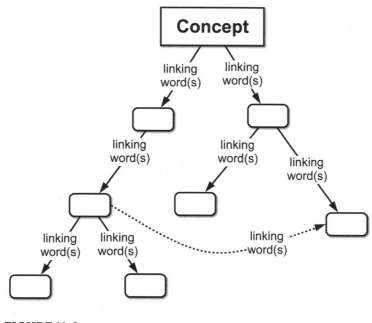

FIGURE 11.6

Cycles

Many topics are best represented as a cycle. These maps provide an
approach to diagramming cycles that can be applied to many curricular areas, from science to cultural studies.

Types of cycles:

Life cycle (of an animal)

Water cycle

Problem-solving cycle

Volcanic eruption

Krebs cycle

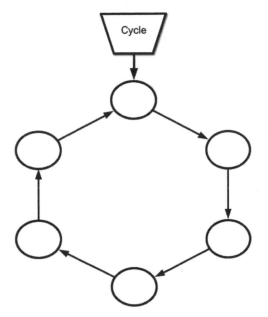

FIGURE 11.7

Vocabulary, Chronology, and Summary

Vocabulary, chronology, and summary are three common areas of study, and these graphic organizers can make teaching and learning them easier.

Frayer Model for Vocabulary

The Frayer Model for vocabulary is a web variant that helps students separate components of a useful definition of a word and gain a deeper understanding by adding pictures, examples, and non-examples (which help establish for the student what the word is *not*).

Word choice can make the difference between writing that is precise and engaging versus vague and dull. Turn the Frayer diagram into a vocabulary expansion activity by asking students to complete each quadrant with synonyms of the central word. They can add images, sentences, and intensity rankings to clarify meaning. For the word "happy," students might add the words "content," "glad," "exuberant," and "elated" to the boxes, and have a discussion about how to rank them 1 to 4 from most happy to least happy.

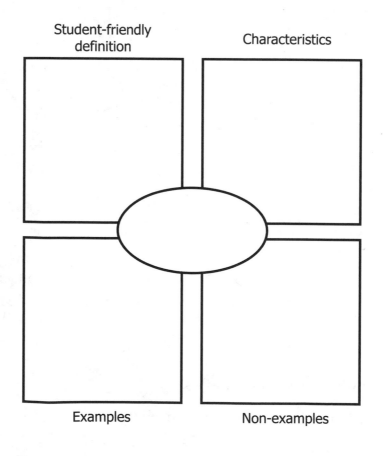

FIGURE 11.8

Chronology Timelines

Timelines offer a clear way to model a sequence of events. A variation on the single timeline (which is not shown) is the dual timeline. Dual timelines help students make sophisticated connections between sequences of events that may occur at different times or in different places. For instance, this type of graphic organizer may be useful to show comparisons between political uprisings. Event 1 in Topic 1 could relate the 1989 Tiananmen Square demonstrations against the Chinese government in Beijing with Event 2 in Topic 2, which could indicate the Selma to Montgomery march of the Civil Rights Movement in 1964. Dual timelines are useful for analyzing parallel progression across surprisingly diverse areas of study. Try using them in science, math, culture, or literature.

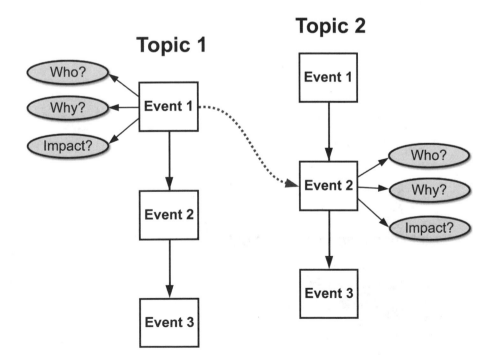

FIGURE 11.9

Summary

There are many ways to organize a summary. Summary Man, explored in chapter 9, is one approach. Another method is the 3–2–1 Summary. The 3-2-1 Summary provides a plan that helps students focus on how to read a text, but it provides the flexibility for students to complete the plan in ways that satisfy their curiosity and personal interest. In doing so, the 3–2–1 Summary engages students in a text in a personally meaningful way rather than asking them to simply recite lists of facts.[3]

A few topics for summary:

Book or book chapter
Scene or movie
Story
Nonfiction event
Scientific process
Article
Play

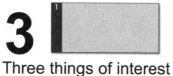

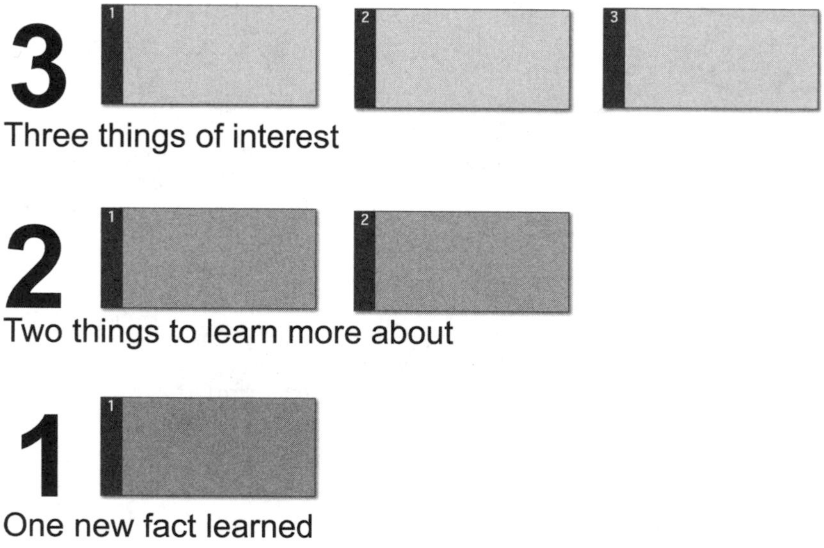

Three things of interest

Two things to learn more about

One new fact learned

FIGURE 11.10

Simple Comparison and Analysis

Analysis is at the heart of critical thinking. These examples that follow provide additional ways to help students organize their ideas and structure their learning to create well-reasoned analyses with appropriate evidence.

Comparison Diagram

Related to the Venn diagram, this graphic organizer offers an alternative method of considering similarities, differences, and overlap between topics using comparison maps.[4]

A few topics for comparing and contrasting:

Two books
Two characters
Plant and animal cells
Two diseases
Two artists
Two authors
Two cities
Two countries
Two cultures

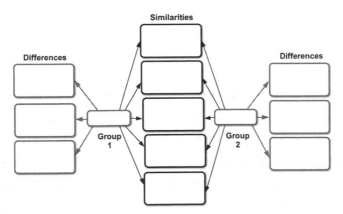

FIGURE 11.11

Analogy Diagram

Similar to vocabulary, analogy is naturally analyzed visually. The diagram below provides a simple approach to model a visual relationship that clarifies a conceptual relationship.[5]

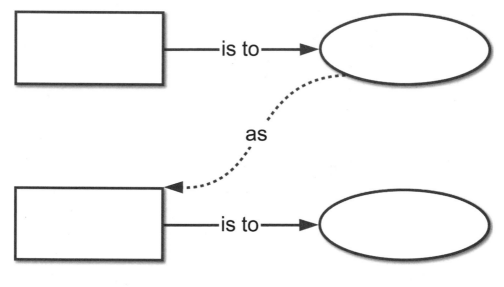

FIGURE 11.12

Cause and Effect

Thinking about causal relationships visually helps students clarify concepts and build logical-thinking skills. The cause and effect diagram also asks students to go beyond identification of effects to predict further implications of the causes and effects being explored. These critical-thinking skills encourage students to be creative, use pertinent evidence to explore concepts, and to think globally about ideas.[6]

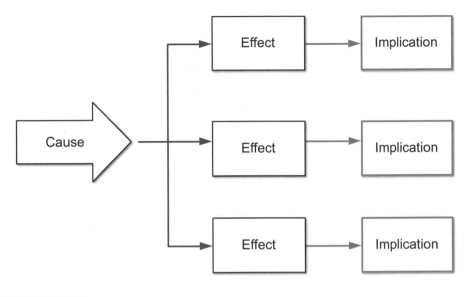

FIGURE 11.13

Point of View Diagram

Analyzing different experiences or events from different points of view is a challenging exercise for students and adults alike. It requires imagination, empathy, and sophisticated understanding. This format can help students to relate to alternative positions and approach ideas from different perspectives. To use this template, insert an event in one of the event bubbles, and insert the contrasting or similar reactions of characters 1 and 2 in the appropriate blanks. For instance, In "Jack and the Beanstalk," Jack might view entering the giant's home as en exciting adventure, while the giant may consider it breaking and entering. This diagram could be effectively used to analyze political or societal events, or any topic for which an analysis from different perspectives can shed new light.[7]

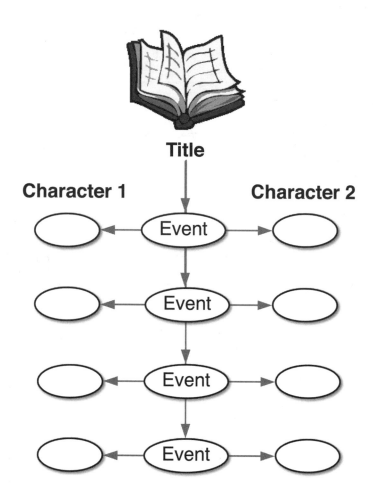

FIGURE 11.14

PCAN Model for Persuasive Speaking

The PCAN (problem, cause, answer, net benefits) model is designed to help develop and deliver a persuasive argument. It provides a method of thinking deeply and analytically about a question, which in turn, strengthens one's ability to articulate the argument. The PCAN diagram is an interpretation of the PCAN Model of Public Speaking from *The Art of Woo* by Mario Moussa. More about this work can be found in the resources section. Use the boxes to prepare your ideas. Then practice performing your persuasive pitch!

Rather than show a blank PCAN template, I've shown how I used the PCAN diagram to prepare a persuasive argument about visual thinking and master a brief, convincing pitch. My PCAN diagram became my thirty-second elevator speech for the Visual Leap, which appears after the diagram below.

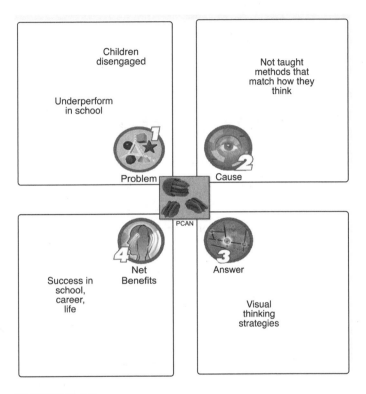

FIGURE 11.15

We have a problem. Millions of our students are disengaged and underperform in school. This has drastic effects on their lives and impacts society as a whole. One cause of this problem is that school focuses on *what to learn*, and not on *how to learn*. Luckily, we can begin to address this today. The answer lies in visual thinking. Students need to be taught how to learn visually because it matches how they naturally think. The net benefits of gaining this skill are immense. By acquiring a better way to learn, students will develop the tools they need to succeed in school, career, and life.

Complex Comparison and Analysis

Teaching students to compare and contrast using evidence is a core skill emphasized in today's Common Core State Standards. Grouping thoughts within a graphical framework helps students to think critically about concepts, focus on parallel construction of ideas, filter out extraneous information, and make reasoned assertions.

Article Comparison Essay Diagram

This diagram helps to organize a comparison essay. It structures the information so students can clearly identify the main points to compare, and it guides their analysis so that the argument will have parallel construction and stay on point.

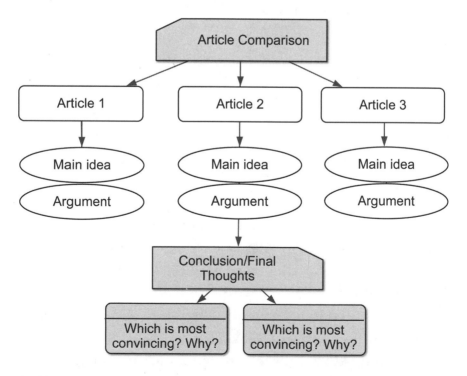

FIGURE 11.16

Event Analysis (Social Studies, Science)

Analyzing events through the lens of causality can help students to see beyond the immediate causes to gain insight into the complexity of events whose original seeds of change or unrest may date back centuries. A former student of mine used this starter template to research the causes of 9/11. This student is particularly special to me because he used this strategy to help return to college after suffering a serious concussion that forced him to withdraw. Visual thinking helped him to organize ideas and grapple with a large project, which had been hard for him to complete since his accident. He used this template and gradually learned that the historical causes of 9/11 went back to clashes between regional groups and the decline of colonialism, and that it was influenced by the Cold War. Some seeds of discord dated back hundreds of years, encompassing wars and ideological battles far more complex than the stories reported in the news.

This work was based on the template that follows, which provides a clear way to visualize and explore causality in a way that promotes critical thinking and layered analysis.[8]

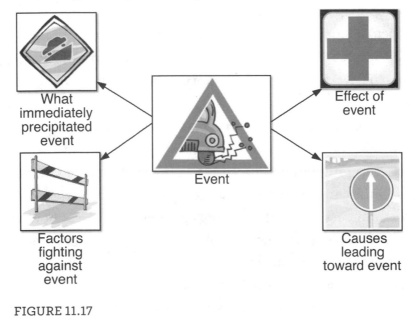

FIGURE 11.17

Allegory Map

Allegory is a simple concept but it often causes confusion or problems with reading comprehension. Not surprisingly, many readers find it hard to follow a nonlinear timeline and to transition between a central storyline and a parallel or tangential storyline or parable. The allegory map is designed to visually depict a story within a story. Concentric rings help the reader see how multiple storylines in a book relate to one another. In the case of allegory, the concentric rings represent the story within a story. Nodes can be placed on any orbital to clarify interconnected events and parallel structures. To create an allegory map, draw concentric circles on an interactive whiteboard, dry-erase board, or piece of paper. Then add any nodes to the rings to depict the story and relationships. Teachers and students can add plot details, timeline events, or even thematically connected events and allusions to the appropriate rings.

The allegory map makes reading more enjoyable and understandable because it helps learners reveal insights that may not be possible without it, which helps them to persevere through challenging texts. To use this map effectively, expect to customize it extensively to suit the particular story. However, maintain the visual metaphor of concentric circles to reinforce the concept of a story within a story. The allegory map below demonstrates the storylines in the book *Holes* by Louis Sachar.[9]

Holes is a beautifully structured book with an engaging plot and a series of interconnected, intergenerational plotlines and themes. The allegory map provides a place to represent the five generations of the Yelnats family and to show how the histories and intrigues of each generation impact the next. The rings also help to reveal how various themes carry through the generations. In reaching the story's zenith, the map helps make it clear how Stanley's heroic final victory resolves generations of unfinished family tragedy and that his victory is also only possible because of the adventures and misadventures of his ancestors.

Stanley's closure brings his ancestors' stories full circle. For some readers, the many rich layers of this book would be lost in the confusion of trying to distinguish all of the different generations. The allegory map brings the beautiful story to full light and provides a vehicle for deep, close, and thoroughly enjoyable reading.

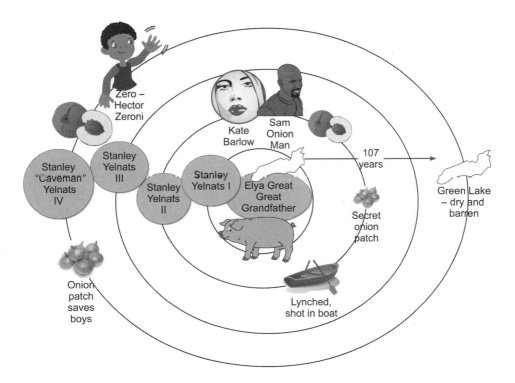

FIGURE 11.18

Ethical Dilemma Diagram

The ethical dilemma diagram pushes students to analyze the pros and cons of difficult choices they may face, gaining a deeper understanding of the different motivations that lead people to act differently in a similar situation. This diagram can help individuals become more open to understanding alternative viewpoints.

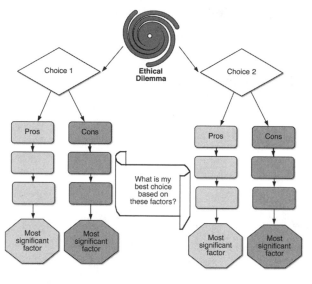

FIGURE 11.19

Web Plan for a Science Lab Report

Preparing a lab report is a taxing new skill for emerging scientists. The web below provides a holistic visualization of scientific method and provides a roadmap to document an experiment.

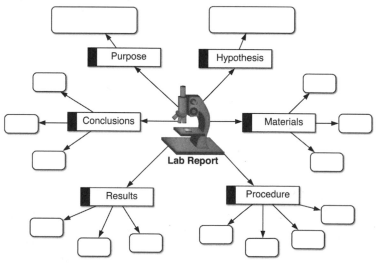

FIGURE 11.20

Mapping in Mathematics

Mapping in mathematics can help students make sense of the questions being asked and can help them understand the processes for solving problems. The examples in this section focus on two areas: word problems and mathematical processes. An entirely different area for classroom integration involves math visualization with virtual interactive manipulatives, such as online number lines, base ten blocks, and virtual geoboards. (I love to work with teachers with virtual manipulatives and hope they will be the topic of a future book.)

Mapping Story Problems in Math

Teachers report that students struggle more with analyzing story problems—to determine the question being asked—than with the actual computation involved. By mapping the question, students can determine what information they have—and what they need to find out. When students begin their approach this way, they can more successfully complete the question. Mapping word problems follows the concepts introduced in chapter 9 in the Web Prompt, which teaches how to deconstruct constructed response prompts. When students are able to break down the question being asked, they can successfully solve it.

Example Story Problem

When Dale babysat for twelve hours and worked at a restaurant for three hours, he made a total of $129. When he babysat for four hours and worked at a restaurant for six hours, he made $78. How much does Dale get paid for each type of work?

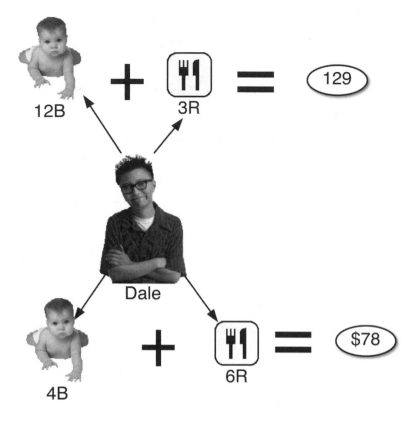

12B   +   3R   =   129

Dale

4B   +   6R   = $78

FIGURE 11.21

Mapping Mathematical Processes

Mathematical concepts can be difficult to understand, and the procedures required to solve math problems can be tricky. Flowcharts can clarify the procedures students need to follow to persevere and successfully solve problems. Asking students to create flowcharts that visualize math procedures goes even further: it provides a level of cognitive engagement that can lead to profound mathematical understanding.

Example 1

Writing the Equation of a Line in the Slope-Intercept Form:
$y = mx + b$

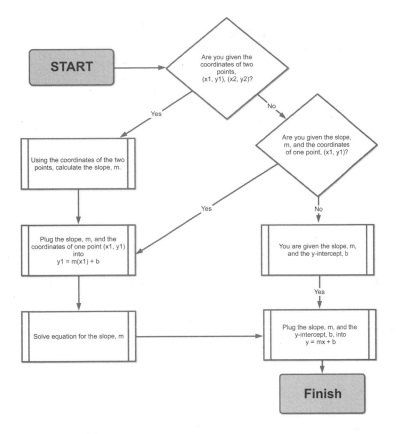

FIGURE 11.22

Personal and Professional Planning

Webs and maps provide an effective way to gain specific academic skills, as well as a natural way to self-monitor learning and create plans to follow. The examples in this section round out the chapter by modeling ways to use visual thinking to plan lessons and to manage a hectic twenty-first-century life.

Lesson Plan

Lesson planning should be one of the most enjoyable parts of teaching, but the way it is often prescribed can seem more like doing taxes. The

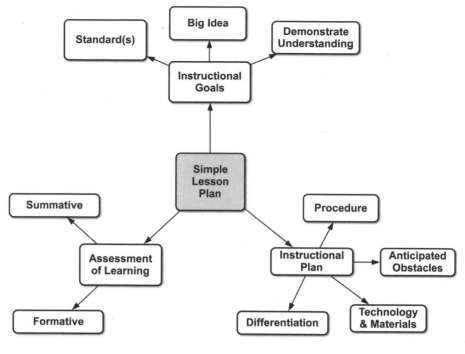

FIGURE 11.23

forms are often detailed and cumbersome. Lesson plan templates seem designed for legal compliance and often stifle creativity. Most of us did not go into teaching because we love paperwork and forms.

Converting planning into a visual act of assembling the puzzle of what and how to teach brings the creativity back into the process. Use this model or design your own to restore pleasure to prep.

My Week

Where did the time go? Often, our weeks seem to evaporate, and we can't figure out where the hours went. This planner lets learners analyze their week, identify the gaps, and get a better sense of how their time is spent. It can also be used as a weekly planner to manage scheduled obligations and determine priorities. I personally use this for overall sanity and life–work balance.

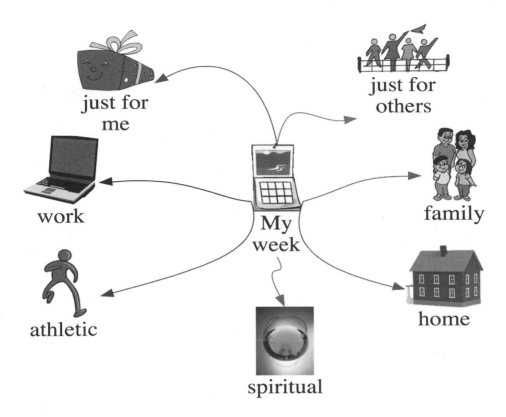

just for
me

just for
others

work

family

My
week

athletic

home

spiritual

FIGURE 11.24

Conclusion

The set of examples throughout this chapter shows visualization strategies for teaching and learning. Use them to inspire, spur creativity, and speed up lesson preparation. Integrating these strategies and developing your own are ideal ways to differentiate instruction and to expand the approaches students use for problem solving and learning. Embrace them because visual thinking is enjoyable and effective. Allow these strategies to give voice and vision to that creative, rule-breaking side of your mind that does not do things in the order it was told. You may be surprised at the impact that it has. Have fun, and thank you for taking the Visual Leap.

RESOURCES

With sincere gratitude I appreciate that you have chosen this book. By doing so, I welcome you into my professional learning community and thank you for welcoming me into yours. As such, I want you to consider me to be your first resource. I am personally available to answer questions you may have about visual thinking and want to discuss how you, your school, or your district can reap the maximum impact of these practices for your students. I gladly welcome your inquiries, suggestions, and comments. Talking with teachers about teaching is my favorite thing to do. Contact me directly so we can take the Visual Leap together. Here is my contact information:

Name:	Jesse Berg
Website:	http://www.visualleap.com
Twitter:	https://twitter.com/visualleap
LinkedIn:	https://www.linkedin.com/in/jesseberg

Downloadable Templates and Online Videos

To access templates, videos, and other resources, please scan the QR code on the next page or visit my website at: http://www.visualleap.com/resources.html.

The remainder of the book presents software, apps, and books that I believe have great professional value. I want to begin, however, by highlighting two special organizations.

Center for Applied Special Technology (CAST) (cast.org)

CAST is a nonprofit education research and development organization dedicated to expanding learning opportunities for all people. CAST developed Universal Design for Learning (UDL), which is a framework for teaching and learning based on the science of human cognition that supports the strategies and methods I have proposed.

International Society for Technology in Education (ISTE) (iste.org)

ISTE is a nonprofit organization dedicated to supporting the use of digital-age tools for teaching and learning. ISTE developed the ISTE NETS standards for teachers, students, instructional coaches, and administrators that have been widely adopted. ISTE conferences, resources, and political advocacy create a coherency to the field of educational technology.

Software and Apps

Advances in science and pedagogy and the advent of the digital age have led to an explosion of amazing visual thinking software, apps, and web tools that enhance learning and productivity. This section identifies select products and resources for visual thinking that have a role in K–12 education. However, it is not a comprehensive list. New entrants appear constantly, and the technology is changing all the time. There are also outstanding visual thinking resources primarily geared toward professional and corporate audiences that are not included here.

Inspiration Software, Inc. (inspiration.com)

A stalwart for decades, Inspiration is the original visual thinking software for education. Inspiration Software offers desktop software, web-based software, and iPad apps geared for K–12 education. The Inspiration family of products is unique because all of its tools allow the user to *simultaneously work with ideas as diagrams and outlines*. By providing users with these two modes for working with ideas, users can create diagrams while thinking "visually" or create outlines while thinking "linearly." Inspiration Software products may be the ultimate tools for convergent and divergent thinking because they seamlessly integrate right-hemispheric visual thinking and left-hemispheric sequential thinking in their products. In my opinion, Inspiration Software products are essential tools for every school. Most of the images and diagrams in this book were created with Inspiration.

Their products include:

- Inspiration (desktop software) for ages 9–99
- Kidspiration (desktop software) for ages 5–10
- Webspiration Classroom (Web-based software)
- Inspiration Maps and Kidspiration Maps (iPad apps)

Kidspiration 3 includes a robust set of exceptional interactive math tools that enable learners to use visualization and modeling to think critically about mathematics, a primary goal of the Common Core State Standards.

Popplet (popplet.com)

Popplet is a mind mapping and webbing tool that exists as **web-based software** and also as an **iPad app**. It may have the most pleasant interface of any of the visual thinking tools being reviewed. Its inviting appearance draws the user in to explore and create. When I do trainings in schools new to visual thinking, I usually choose Popplet because teachers learn to use it instantly, and it easily can perform all of the key instructional procedures in this book like the Webstorm, Reverse Mind Map, and Summary Man.

It is inviting and easy to use, making it a great tool for students and teachers to quickly jump in and use. It also packs in serious features. For instance, Popplet accepts images, text, hand drawings, and videos that can be embedded from YouTube and Vimeo. It is designed for online collaboration. Not only can different users work on the same "popple" (their word for a Popplet diagram) online, but popples can be shared publicly, so there is a large variety of searchable Popplet webs and diagrams to use in class. Popplet continues to rapidly evolve as a premier mapping tool that is highly appropriate for use in K–12 education. Popplet even offers a good free trial version.

Ideament iPad App (nosleep.net)

The Ideament app lets users easily develop mind maps and webs as diagrams and outlines. Like Inspiration tools, with Ideament, the user can simultaneously toggle between both views to work in whichever modality is more comfortable at a given time. It also offers multiple export modes, so files are easy to share. Many of the strategies in this book could easily and effectively be done with iPads with the Ideament app, as it is similar to the Inspiration Maps app in terms of the core functionality of webbing and outlining.

iMindMap (thinkbuzan.com)

iMindMap software and iPad app need to be on any list of standout mind-mapping resources because of the rich visualization capabilities—and because they were developed by Tony Buzan, inventor of the term "mind map." iMindMap stands out among its peers because it provides more robust tools for rich visual representation and artistic embellishment than other mind-mapping software. The reason for this emphasis is tied to the philosophy of iMindmap. Based on Tony Buzan's research, the most useful mind maps for comprehension, recall, and communication are deeply expressive and individualistic creations. Therefore, this family of tools focuses on bringing the benefits of hand-drawn mind maps to the digital experience.

iMindMap software comes in several models depending on the target audience. The home and student tool is mentioned here, but they also offer an enterprise version with business-oriented features and Gantt charts. Like the best visual thinking tools, iMindMap offers simultaneous outline and diagram views, as well as some other creative 3-D interpretations and visually impressive presentation modes. The other unique workspace in iMindmap is what is akin to a digital bulletin board. It is a space where you can drag and drop virtually any file or media into a freeform workspace. This is a new approach to building a project that breaks down the barriers of files and folders to offer people a more organic approach to conceptualizing and planning an idea. The iMindMap iPad app allows for mind maps to be created and shared, but the more dynamic features require a subscription membership.

RealtimeBoard (realtimeboard.com)

RealtimeBoard is a truly unique subscription-based collaborative web tool that is similar to the digital bulletin board mode of iMindmap. Unlike iMindmap, RealtimeBoard works directly in a browser window in Firefox, Safari, or Chrome. It is like having a multi-dimensional bulletin board that transcends time and space by allowing users to collaborate dynamically. In this space, participants can create mind maps, free-form diagrams, upload documents to share, and more. Since it is fully collaborative and seamlessly integrated with cloud storage services like Drive and Dropbox, it becomes a totally flexible environment to share and work visually. Anybody with access can add their ideas and contribute to a discussion with comments, images, videos, and basically any type of media imaginable.

RealtimeBoard feels like a completely new and different type of environment for thinking, working, and collaborating. It is easy to use, has a gorgeous and intuitive interface, and using it feels like being on the cutting edge of something special and transformative. If I were giving an award for New, Cool, and Useful, RealtimeBoard might just win.

Coggle (coggle.it)

Coggle is an intriguing new web-based mind-mapping application that is notable for several reasons. First, it is free and promises to stay that way forever. Second, it is firmly integrated with Google Apps. Therefore, to install Coggle, one needs simply to go to the Chrome Web Store (chrome.google.com/webstore) to find and install it. Coggle will then be associated with the user's Google account, and sharing and collaboration can be established by inviting others. Once it is installed, Coggle can also be used in all major web browsers. Coggle is not Flash-based, so it actually works pretty well in the lightweight browsers on iPads and Android tablets. If total cross-platform flexibility (iPad/Android tablet/Mac/PC) is a consideration, Coggle is the rare tool that offers this capability at this point in time.

Coggle is simple and has basic functions you would expect, such as the ability to produce hierarchically structured documents, but at this time it lacks the more sophisticated features that other tools offer. It also hides some of its advanced features to preserve a clean user interface. Coggle does not support simultaneous webbing and outlining like Idea Flip or Inspiration, but it has an active community that is working to improve it. The API (application program interface) is available for developers, and the team behind Coggle seems to embody the collaborative spirit of the early days of the Internet. If you want total cross-platform, cross-device compatibility and don't have any money for mind-mapping software and never will, and if you do not want to be limited by the restrictions of *freemium* software, then Coggle is worth a close look.

The Math Learning Center (mathlearningcenter.org)

The Math Learning Center (MLC) is known for their outstanding math curricula, but my favorite gems are their virtual math manipulative apps and web tools. Their online geoboard, base ten blocks, number line, and pattern blocks are just a few of their simply perfect tools. They allow students to explore and model a diverse array of mathematical concepts and to build problem-solving skills. Their cross-platform apps are wonderful, flexible, and free! Since I have started following and using their tools, MLC has added several new ones. Android tablet, laptop, and computer users can access their web tools through browsers. iPad users can download their free tools as apps from iTunes. These outstanding manipulatives significantly enhance the study of mathematics through mathematical modeling, which is a core component of the Common Core State Standards. MLC virtual manipulatives should be in every teacher's tool kit. (To download or access these tools, go to catalog.mathlearningcenter.org/apps.)

Brainingcamp (brainingcamp.com)

Brainingcamp is a subscription-based math curriculum that also provides excellent virtual math manipulative apps for iPad, and web tools for PC or Mac. Without purchasing their entire curriculum, users can find Brainingcamp apps in the iTunes store at a very reasonable price, and Brainingcamp often offers apps for free. Like the Math Learning Center resources, these apps allow a teacher or student to explore math concepts visually. In contrast, many of their apps also include instructional lessons that logically step students through the concept being introduced and help a teacher to present concepts. The clean interface and open-ended qualities of their tools distinguish them from drill-and-practice type apps that focus on mastery through repetition or memorization. A few of their tools include algebra tiles, pattern blocks, color tiles, histograms, number lines, and number rods.

Math Playground (mathplayground.com)

Math Playground is a popular learning site filled with math games, logic puzzles, step-by-step instructional videos, math practice, and a variety of problem-solving activities. It provides a safe place for kids to learn and explore math concepts online. Math Playground works on the full-function browsers in laptops and desktops, but they are also developing more and more apps for iPad.

National Library of Virtual Manipulatives (NLVM) (nlvm.usu.edu) and Matti Math (mattimath.com)

The National Library of Virtual Manipulatives is a free online resource with over 100 virtual manipulative math tools for K-12 educators. It was developed by Utah State University and funded by the National Science Foundation. This Java-based repository is dated in its appearance and wonky, but the tools are great for teaching diverse math topics. It also provides guidelines on how to use the tools. Base ten blocks, algebra tiles, and tessellations are a few of their resources. NLVM is beginning to migrate to the tablet world. They are associated with Matti Math, which sells NLVM tools as desktop software for Windows and Mac. This partnership delivers powerful online and offline visual learning resource for teaching and learning math.

More Excellent Visual Thinking Tools

There are too many excellent visual thinking tools on the market to describe in detail in this book, and new ones are entering all the time. That said, I could not leave these off the list.

Mindjet (mindjet.com) is a popular and versatile professional mind-mapping tool, with web tool and app products. It has unique calculation features suitable to project budgeting and mathematical analysis that work within the visual structure of a mind map. You can see the financial implications of different scenarios immediately. Amazing!

Mindmeister (mindmeister.com) is designed for collaboration. It is accessible from any platform (iPad, Android, laptop), has numerous options for presentation, and offers many ways to export and share files.

TheBrain (thebrain.com) is a dynamic professional mind-mapping software and app with a distinctive interface and a unique approach to visualizing thinking. With TheBrain, any node can become a main topic by clicking on it. Through an animation, that node becomes the main topic, and anything attached becomes a subtopic. It is a powerful approach to associative thinking and promotes exploration of ideas.

XMind (xmind.net) is a professional and powerful mind-mapping software, complemented by web tool and app products. XMind offers many visual thinking template starters that go beyond mind maps and include timelines, outline views, Gantt chart views, and more.

Mindomo (mindomo.com) tools place an emphasis on collaboration and creating a consistent user experience. The desktop and browser versions of the software are basically identical, and Mindomo offers

both an iPad and Android app. One of the best features of the Mindomo suite is the ability to embed multimedia such as video from You-
Tube or Vimeo, or to link to images on Flickr.

Books

Any work I have done in the space of visual thinking, multi-sensory
learning, Universal Design for Learning, ADHD, dyslexia, autism spectrum disorders, and instructional technology has not been done alone.
A wonderful community of educators, researchers, writers, and software developers has helped me every day in all of my efforts. The next
few pages highlight a few essential works for anyone trying to learn
more about visual thinking and learning, plus a few extras that have
informed my practice or enlightened me professionally.

Upside-Down Brilliance: The Visual-Spatial Learner by Linda Kreger Silverman. Denver: DeLeon Publishing, 2002.

Linda Kreger Silverman is the founder and director of the Institute for
the Study of Advanced Development and its subsidiaries, Gifted Development Center (GDC) and Visual-Spatial Resource, in Denver, Colorado (www.gifteddevelopment.com). Among other things, she coined
the terms "visual-spatial learner" and "auditory-sequential learner." Her
research spawned a cottage industry of books and generated a much
deeper understanding of visual-spatial learning, giftedness, and the
diverse needs of all learners.

Upside-Down Brilliance gracefully presents a summary of Silverman's
years of research in an accessible way that non-researchers will understand and that researchers will find compelling. It then uses her find-
ings to explain how to work with visual learners in the classroom. This

is the original book about visual-spatial learning, and one from which both teachers and parents can benefit from immensely.

Mapping the Mind by Rita Carter. Los Angeles: University of California Press, 2000.

Mapping the Mind brings science and art together in a book that illuminates the human history of cognitive development. Rita Carter explains the evolution and the function of the mind as much through story and illustration as through her astute analysis of scientific writing. Leading experts contribute engaging stories throughout the book, highlighting bizarre and hysterical examples of human behavior (like the condition of "alien hand") that exemplify the inner workings—or lack thereof—of the mind. The result is a fascinating explanation of how people think, learn, and interact. Carter's book contains beautiful color diagrams and illustrations that support her examples. Reading this book is a multisensory experience that is a visual, tactile, and intellectual feast.

The Shut-Down Learner by Richard Selznick, PhD. Boulder, CO: Sentient Publications, 2008.

The first book written by Richard Selznick, *The Shut-Down Learner* is based on Selznick's clinical experiences as director of Cooper Learning Center of Cooper Hospital in New Jersey. He coined this term to shed light on the painful and debilitating scholastic experiences of the large numbers of his patients who excelled at visual and spatial tasks while struggling with core academic tasks like reading and writing. This book is primarily directed toward parents, and it presents complicated data in a straightforward manner. *The Shut-Down Learner* offers clear guidelines that can strengthen home and school relationships in order to help academically frustrated at-risk students.

Right-Brained Children in a Left-Brained World: Unlocking the Potential of Your ADD Child by Jeffrey Freed, MAT, and Laurie Parsons. New York: Simon & Schuster, 1998.

This is one of the first—and one of the most thorough—books dealing with the topic of right-hemispheric thinking and ADHD. Freed and Parsons provide a detailed and clear account of the left-brain and right-brain dichotomy and offer simple checklist-style inventories to help uncover the learning needs of children. Then they go on to deliver detailed practical strategies for teaching nearly every academic subject and skill, including spelling, reading, math, and writing. The book delivers insight on effective approaches to discipline and even weighs in on the debate over medication for individuals diagnosed with ADHD. For many parents and educators, myself included, this is one of the most well-worn resource books in the library because the information remains so useful and timeless.

A Whole New Mind: Why Right-Brainers Will Rule the Future by Daniel H. Pink. New York: Riverhead, 2006.

In *A Whole New Mind*, Dan Pink takes the right-brain discussion out of education and places it in a societal and economic context. He presents the compelling argument of why our right-brain, visual-thinking, creative types are essential for America's continuing prosperity. Pink argues that qualities of the left-brain thinkers—organization and accuracy—that were essential to prosperity in the "Information Age" of knowledge workers have become commodities in the present "Conceptual Age." Pink reports that these left-brain qualities and the jobs that require them have already been exported because they can be done more cheaply or better by technology or through outsourcing. Therefore, the remaining opportunities for the post–Information Age lie in innovative thinking, the search for meaning, and the ability to design and create. These are the skills of the right-brainer. Wow! With an argument like that, Pink gives every frustrated, insecure, shut-down learner a huge dose of confidence and the spitfire and gumption to go conquer the world.

Visual Tools for Transforming Information into Knowledge, 2nd edition, by David N. Hyerle. Thousand Oaks, CA: Corwin, 2008.

David Hyerle is a ninja master of visual thinking. This comprehensive work manages the rare feat of being at once scholarly and practical. It explains the science of learning and provides a firm research foundation for visual tools and strategies that can be used to meet diverse learning objectives. Hyerle illuminates subtle differences between graphic organizers, as well as details their uses in education and industry. For educators, the book provides guidelines to help implement visual tools successfully in classes. Hyerle believes in the need for students to take ownership of their learning, and a central argument he makes is for a consistent and cohesive approach to teaching students the way they think and learn. What makes this book so unusual, however, is that he provides clear and useful guidelines for this transformation in the form of checklists and rubrics, which make this all seem possible and too important to ignore.

Use Both Sides of Your Brain: New Mind-Mapping Techniques, 3rd edition, by Tony Buzan. New York: Plume, 1991.

Any book about visual thinking should honor Tony Buzan, the mind behind mind mapping. Buzan is an innovator in learning techniques, and his work spawned the industry of mind-mapping tools. He is one of the most significant voices in the dialogue about right-brain learning. In *Use Both Sides of Your Brain*, Buzan presents his theory of radial thinking. He follows with practical strategies to read faster and with greater comprehension, to remember longer, and to problem-solve complex questions. The book contains the rules for mind mapping and suggests many different contexts in which to apply the techniques in order to use our brains to the best advantage.

The Gift of Dyslexia: Why Some of the Smartest People Can't Read...and How They Can Learn, revised and expanded edition, by Ronald D. Davis. New York: Perigee Trade, 2010.

Ronald Davis explains dyslexia in a new light. He describes the condition as "a natural ability, a talent." Unfortunately, this "talent" can cause debilitating problems in school such as frustration, isolation, and low self-esteem. However, the same talent makes dyslexics highly intuitive, insightful, and curious. They think mainly in pictures, not words. Davis explains that many of the reading difficulties people with dyslexia experience, in fact, come from disorientation that results from not having a mental picture for a given word. In *The Gift of Dyslexia*, Davis explains how the reading problem can be corrected, and how the intrinsic creativity of the dyslexic can lead to extraordinary accomplishments that may not otherwise be possible. This is an illuminating and positive book that may make some folks wish they had dyslexia.

Mapping Inner Space: Learning and Teaching Visual Mapping by Nancy Margulies with Nusa Maal. Tucson: Zephyr Press, 2002.

Mapping Inner Space is a gorgeous how-to book for mind mapping. Its illustrations would motivate even the most reluctant to embrace visual thinking. Margulies covers strategies to capture ideas and begin to freely draw a visual mental map that guides the hand. Numerous classroom examples are provided, in addition to steps that beginning visual thinkers can take to express their ideas. This book is a delight to browse and peruse.

The Back of the Napkin by Dan Roam. New York: Penguin Group, 2009.

This best-selling book may have, more than any other, brought visual thinking to the forefront as a problem-solving strategy in the American business community. Roam provides a roadmap for visual thinking in this superb, simple, elegant, and engaging business book. What I strive to do for school-age students, Dan Roam has done countless times over with Fortune 100 CEOs. His gift for revealing complex problems with simple visualizations underscores his genius. This book will inspire you to think visually, and it provides specific approaches about how to do so. *The Back of the Napkin* belongs in any visual thinker's library.

My Stroke of Insight: A Brain Scientist's Personal Journey by Jill Bolte Taylor. New York: Penguin Group, 2008.

All of the books about right-hemispheric thinking, left-hemispheric thinking, and the traits of both take a backseat to *My Stroke of Insight*. None of them will give you a fraction of the understanding of thinking and the human mind that this book will. The reason is because the author, Jill Bolte Taylor, a brain scientist at Harvard, wrote about her personal experience of having a massive stroke on the left side of her brain. As blood flooded her left hemisphere, quieting it for years, she experienced the essence of right-brain thinking because that was all she was capable of—and she loved it. Her profound and inspiring account of her injury and recovery is written with the scientific under-standing of an expert, yet this first person account intimately reveals the true human experience of how our two minds work together to create the people we are. I am quite sure that this book changed my outlook on life and my professional practice forever.

The Reason I Jump: The Inner Voice of a Thirteen-Year-Old Boy with Autism by Naoki Higashida, translated by KA Yoshida and David Mitchell. New York: Random House, 2013.

The Reason I Jump occupies the same rarified air as *My Stroke of Insight* by providing a window into human thinking from inside an exceptional mind. *The Reason I Jump* is written by Naoki Higashida, a thirteen-year-old boy with autism. He explains how his addled mind tries to make sense of the world, and he shares his immense compassion and appreciation for those who help him learn how to function in a world that his mind doesn't want to cooperate with. Working with an inspiring and outstanding group of teachers at a school for autism recently, I shared the following quote from this book:

> But I ask you, those of you who are with us all day, not to stress yourselves out because of us. When you do this, it feels as if you're denying any value at all that our lives may have—and that saps the spirit we need to soldier on. The hardest ordeal for us is the idea that we are causing grief for other people. We can put up with our own hardships okay, but the thought that our lives are the source of other people's unhappiness, that's plain unbearable.

After they read the passage, a somber quiet fell over the group. Even with their vast experience and profound well of empathy and patience, they gained an insight they had never had from these words—from a child who could have been their student. Everyone should read this book.

The Art of Woo: Using Strategic Persuasion to Sell Your Ideas by G. Richard Shell and Mario Moussa. New York: Penguin Group, 2007.

The Art of Woo is neither a teaching book, nor a visual learning book. However, listening to Moussa lecture on the topic of his book inspired me to push my hypothesis about mind mapping to the limit, by mind mapping his entire book. (See figure 10.3) Though written for business professionals, this book is relevant for teachers because teaching is also a game of persuasion. In particular, the visual PCAN model that I created based on Shell and Moussa's process is ideal for teaching any student how to speak clearly and construct powerful arguments. Speaking and listening are central tenets of the Common Core State Standards, and more generally, necessary skills for effective communication and success in career and life.

Learning Outside the Lines by Jonathan Mooney and David Cole. New York: Simon and Schuster, 2000.

With chapter titles like "Less Reading, More A's" and "Beating the Exam Game," it is easy to understand how this academic survival story became a learning bible for that most complex character—the learner who seems so smart but for whom school just doesn't quite work. This book is the product of two college misfits who found each other, and a way to overcome obstacles and even thrive in an atmosphere that was not designed to enable their success. After living through debilitating school experiences that nearly broke both of these men with ADHD and dyslexia, they managed to find themselves in college and craft one of the funniest, most useful, and most inspiring learning books ever written. This honest and hysterical book shares their academic misadventures and provides an extensive set of practical tools and strategies that worked for them, will work for others, and which validate the intelligence and potential of their fellow *unusual learners*.

NOTES

Chapter 1

1. *Graphic Organizers: A Review of Scientifically Based Research*, report prepared for Inspiration Software (The Institute for the Advancement of Research in Education (IARE) at AEL, 2003), accessed May 20, 2015, http://www.inspiration.com/Resources/Research.

Chapter 2

1. Rita Carter, *Mapping the Mind* (Los Angeles: University of California Press, 2010), 14.

2. David H. Rose and Anne Meyer, *Teaching Every Student in the Digital Age: Universal Design for Learning* (Alexandria, Virginia: ASCD, 2002), 12.

3. Ibid, 38.

4. Rita Carter, *Mapping the Mind* (Los Angeles: University of California Press, 2010), 111.

5. Ahmad Al-Issa, "Schema Theory and L2 Reading Comprehension: Implications for Teaching," *Journal of College Teaching and Learning* 3, no. 7 (2006): 41.

6. Barbara K. Given, *Teaching to the Brain's Natural Learning Systems* (Alexandria, Virginia: ASCD, 2002), 68.

7. "Sight, Hearing, Braille, Thinking. Colored Positron Emission Tomography (PET) Scans of Areas of the Human Brain Activated by Different Tasks," Wellcome Dept. of Cognitive Neurology/Science Photo Library.

8. Mark Sadoski and Allan Paivio, *Imagery and Text: A Dual Coding Theory of Reading and Writing*, 2nd ed. (New York: Routledge, 2013), 28.

9. Mark Sadoski and Allan Paivio, *Imagery and Text: A Dual Coding Theory of Reading and Writing*, 2nd ed. (New York: Routledge, 2013), 69.

10. James M. Clark and Allan Paivio, "Dual Coding Theory and Education," *Educational Psychology Review* 3, no. 3 (1991): 166.

11. Rita Carter, *Mapping the Mind* (Los Angeles: University of California Press, 2010), 17.

12. Rosalie P. Fink, "Successful Careers: The Secrets of Adults with Dyslexia,"Career Planning & Adult Development Network, accessed April 30, 2015, http://dyslexiahelp.umich.edu/sites/default/files/SuccessfulCareersDyslexiaFink.pdf.

13. Rita Carter, *Mapping the Mind* (Los Angeles: University of California Press, 2010), 32, 175; Francesco d'Errico et al, "Archaeological Evidence for the Emergence of Language, Symbolism, and Music—An Alternative Multidisciplinary Perspective," *Journal of World Prehistory* 17, no. 1 (March 2003): 55.

Chapter 3

1. "For the Blind, Connected Devices Create a Novel Way to Read" (includes an interview with Judy Dixon), by Audie Cornish, *All Things Considered*, January 3, 2014, accessed April 27, 2015, http://www.npr.org/player/v2/media Player.html?action=1&t=1&islist=false&id=259414937&m=259533084.

2. Linda Kreger Silverman, *Upside-Down Brilliance* (Denver: DeLeon Publishing, 2002), 332.

3. Robert W. Weisberg, *Creativity: Understanding Innovation in Problem Solving, Science, Invention, and the Arts* (Hoboken: John Wiley & Sons), 96.

4. Edward de Bono, *Six Thinking Hats* (New York: Back Bay Books), 1999.

5. Linda Kreger Silverman, *Upside-Down Brilliance* (Denver: DeLeon Publishing, 2002), 99.

6. Jonathan Mooney and David Cole, *Learning Outside the Lines* (New York: Simon & Schuster, 2000).

7. Linda Kreger Silverman, *Upside-Down Brilliance* (Denver: DeLeon Publishing, 2002).

8. Richard Selznick, *The Shut-Down Learner* (Boulder: Sentient Publications, 2009).

9. Richard Selznick, *The Shut-Down Learner* (Boulder: Sentient Publications, 2009).

10. Ilene Raymond Rush, "Restoring Right-Brain Activities to Medical School," *Philadelphia Inquirer,* June 15, 2014, accessed Nov. 10, 2014, http://articles.philly .com/2014-06-15/news/50600582_1_burnout-medical-students-salvatore -mangione.

11. Helena Westerberg et al, "Visuo-Spatial Working Memory Span: A Sensitive Measure of Cognitive Deficits in Children With ADHD," *Child Neuropsychology* 10, no. 3 (2004): 155–161.

12. Naoki Higashida, *The Reason I Jump,* trans. KA Yoshida and David Mitchell (New York: Random House), 2013, 71.

13. James Flavell, "Metacognition and Cognitive Monitoring: A New Area of Cognitive–Developmental Inquiry," *American Psychologist,* 34, no. 10 (1979): 908.

Chapter 4

1. PRC AAC Language Lab. "Core Vocabulary." Accessed July 20, 2015. https:// aaclanguagelab.com/resources/core-vocabulary.

Chapter 6

1. Information is based on text in *DK Eyewitness Travel Guide: Hawaii* (New York: Dorling-Kindersley, 2013), 95.

2. Digital Photography School. "What the Mona Lisa Can Teach You About Taking Great Portraits." Accessed July 20, 2015. http://digital-photography -school.com/what-the-mona-lisa-can-teach-you-about-taking-great-portraits/.

Chapter 8

1. Persuasive essay diagram based on an Inspiration Software template, adapted with permission by Inspiration Software, Inc.

2. Project plan diagram based on an Inspiration Software template, adapted with permission by Inspiration Software, Inc.

Chapter 9

1. "Reading Item and Scoring Sampler Grade 11," The Pennsylvania System of School Assessment 2006–2007, Pennsylvania Department of Education Bureau of Assessment and Accountability, 2006–2007, 22–27.

2. "Reading Item and Scoring Sampler Grade 11," The Pennsylvania System of School Assessment 2006–2007, Pennsylvania Department of Education Bureau of Assessment and Accountability 2006–2007, 8–12.

Chapter 10

1. "Dan Pink Office Hours with Biz Stone, Co-founder of Twitter and Author of *Things a Little Bird Told Me: Confessions of the Creative Mind*," narrated by Daniel H. Pink, July 1, 2014, accessed May 2, 2015, http://www.danpink .com/office-hours/biz-stone.

Chapter 11

1. Mind map based on Inspiration Software template, adapted with permission by Inspiration Software, Inc.

2. Concept map diagram based on an Inspiration Software template, adapted with permission by Inspiration Software, Inc.

3. 3–2–1 Summary graphic organizer based on a Sublime Learning template, adapted and reprinted with permission from Sublime Learning, Inc.

4. Comparison diagram based on an Inspiration Software template, adapted with permission by Inspiration Software, Inc.

5. Analogy diagram based on an Inspiration Software template, adapted with permission by Inspiration Software, Inc.

6. Cause and Effect diagram based on an Inspiration Software template, adapted with permission by Inspiration Software, Inc.

7. Point of View diagram based on an Inspiration Software template, adapted with permission by Inspiration Software, Inc.

8. Causality diagram based on an Inspiration Software template, adapted with permission by Inspiration Software, Inc.

9. Louis Sachar, *Holes* (New York: Farrar, Straus and Giroux, 1998).

INDEX

ACKNOWLEDGMENTS

Thank you to Amy, my wife, for enduring the years I have spent working on this book. You are the quintessential finisher to my never-ending process. Thank you to the capable and daring team at my publisher, Lamprey & Lee, for everything, but most specifically for connecting me with Susan Lauzau. Susan's edits helped me shape and refine the manuscript, as only a talented editor and patient teacher could.

Finally, I want to thank the students and educators with whom I have had the honor of working over the years. You have inspired me, motivated me, challenged me, and provided much of the insight that fills these pages. I could not have done this without you.

ABOUT THE AUTHOR

Jesse Berg, MSIT, MEd, is an accomplished teacher, professional coach, instructional technologist, and educational speaker. He began his career as a Spanish teacher and became increasingly drawn into educational technology as he saw the power of simple tools and methods to help individuals make discoveries and breakthroughs in their own learning.

In 2007, Jesse left the classroom to found Visual Leap, which is a mission-driven company dedicated to enhancing teaching practice and student learning with visual thinking strategies that make complex tasks like reading, writing, mathematics, and critical thinking easier to do.

Berg's experience working with public, private, suburban, urban, Parochial and charter schools, as a classroom teacher, instructional coach, educational consultant, speaker, and author inform his practical, student-centered methods. His goal is to work with teachers, administrators, and students to simplify the process of teaching and learning in clear and easy ways that get powerful, lasting results in school, and that remain with students as go-to learning strategies that last a lifetime.

Jesse lives in Philadelphia with his wife, Amy, teenagers Leo and Sophie, and Daphne the family dog.